THE CAREER IDEAS FOR KIDS SERIES

Second Edition

DIANE LINDSEY REEVES
with
LINDSEY CLASEN

Illustrations by
NANCY BOND

Ferguson
An imprint of Infobase Publishing

CAREER IDEAS FOR KIDS WHO LIKE SPORTS, Second Edition

Ferguson
An imprint of Infobase Publishing
132 West 31st Street
New York NY 10001

Library of Congress Cataloging-in-Publication Data

Reeves, Diane Lindsey, 1959–
  Career ideas for kids who like sports / Diane Lindsey Reeves with Lindsey Clasen; illustrations by Nancy Bond. — 2nd ed.
    p. cm — (The career ideas for kids series)
  Includes bibliographical references and index.
  ISBN-13: 978-0-8160-6551-6 (hc : alk. paper)
  ISBN-10: 0-8160-6551-9 (hc : alk. paper) 1. Sports—Vocational guidance—United States—Juvenile literature. I. Clasen, Lindsey. II. Bond, Nancy, ill. III. Reeves, Diane Lindsey, 1959– Science. IV. Title. V. Series.
  GV734.R44 2007
  796.023—dc22   2007002486

Ferguson books are available at special discounts when purchased in bulk quantities for businesses, associations, institutions, or sales promotions. Please call our Special Sales Department in New York at (212) 967-8800 or (800) 322-8755.

You can find Ferguson on the World Wide Web at http://www.fergpubco.com

Original text and cover design by Smart Graphics
Illustrations by Nancy Bond

Printed in the United States of America

MP Hermitage 10 9 8 7 6 5 4 3 2 1

This book is printed on acid-free paper.

CONTENTS

ACKNOWLEDGMENTS

A million thanks to the people who took the time to share their career stories and provide photos for this book:

Debbie Becker
Bob Beretta
Tommy Bowden
Julie Cook
Richard DeLuca
Abby Derman
Jackie Fink
Chad Foster
Joann Francis
Kevin Kahn
Doug Levy
Jim Maurer
Dick Ratliff
Van Tate
Lionel Washington

Finally, much appreciation and admiration is due to all the behind-the-scenes people at Ferguson who have done so much to make this series all that it is. With extra thanks to James Chambers and Sarah Fogarty.

MAKE A CHOICE!

Choices.

You make them every day. What do I want for breakfast? Which shirt can I pull out of the dirty-clothes hamper to wear to school today? Should I finish my homework or play video games?

Some choices don't make much difference in the overall scheme of things. Face it; who really cares whether you wear the blue shirt or the red one?

Other choices are a major big deal. Figuring out what you want to be when you grow up is one of those all-important choices.

But, you say, you're just a kid. How are you supposed to know what you want to do with your life?

You're right: 10, 11, 12, and even 13 are a bit young to know exactly what and where and how you're going to do whatever it is you're going to do as an adult. But it's the perfect time to start making some important discoveries about who you are, what you like to do, and what you do best. It's a great time to start exploring the options and experimenting with different ideas. In fact, there's never a better time to mess around with different career ideas without messing up your life.

When it comes to picking a career, you've basically got two choices.

CHOICE A

You can be like lots of other people and just go with the flow. Float through school doing only what you absolutely have to in order to graduate, take any job you can find, collect a paycheck, and meander your way to retirement without making much of a splash in life.

Although many people take this route and do just fine, others end up settling for second best. They miss out on a meaningful education, satisfying work, and the rewards of a focused and well-planned career. That's why this path is not an especially good idea for someone who actually wants to have a life.

CHOICE B

Other people get a little more involved in choosing a career. They figure out what they want to accomplish in their lives—whether it's making a difference, making lots of money, or simply enjoying what they do. Then they find out what it takes to reach that goal, and they set about doing it with gusto. It's kind of like these people do things on purpose instead of letting life happen by accident.

Choosing A is like going to an ice cream parlor where there are all kinds of awesome flavors and ordering a single scoop of plain vanilla. Going with Choice B is more like visiting that same ice cream parlor and ordering a super duper brownie sundae drizzled with hot fudge, smothered in whip cream, and topped with a big red cherry.

Do you see the difference?

Reading this book is a great idea for kids who want to go after life in a big way. It provides a first step toward learning about careers that match your skills, values, and dreams. It will help you make the most out of your time in school and maybe even inspire you to—as the U.S. Army so proudly says—"be all that you can be."

Ready for the challenge of Choice B? If so, read the next section for instructions on how to get started.

HOW TO USE THIS BOOK

This book isn't just about interesting careers that other people have. It's also a book about interesting careers that you can have.

Of course, it won't do you a bit of good to just read this book. To get the whole shebang, you're going to have to jump in with both feet, roll up your sleeves, put on your thinking cap—whatever it takes—to help you do these three things:

○ Discover what you do best and enjoy the most. (This is the secret ingredient for finding work that's perfect for you.)

☼ Explore ways to match your interests and abilities with career ideas.

☼ Experiment with lots of different ideas until you find the ideal career. (It's like trying on all kinds of hats to see which ones fit!)

Use this book as a road map to some exciting career destinations. Here's what to expect in the chapters that follow.

GET IN GEAR!

First stop: discover. These activities will help you uncover important clues about the special traits and abilities that make you *you*. When you are finished you will have developed a personal Skill Set that will help guide you to career ideas in the next chapter.

TAKE A TRIP!

Next stop: explore. Cruise down the career idea highway and find out about a variety of career ideas that are especially appropriate for people who like sports. Use the Skill Set chart at the beginning of each career profile to match your own interests with those required for success on the job.

Once you've identified a career that interests you, kick your exploration into high gear by checking out some of the Web sites, library resources, and professional organizations listed at the end of each career profile. For an extra challenge, follow the instructions for the Try It Out activities.

MAKE A SPORTY DETOUR!

Here's your chance to explore up-and-coming opportunities in athletics and fitness as well as the related fields of recreation, sports information, and athlete representation.

Just when you thought you'd seen it all, here come dozens of sports ideas to add to the career mix. Charge up your

DISCOVER #2: RULES OF THE ROAD

Pretty much any job you can think of involves six common ingredients. Whether the work requires saving the world or selling bananas, all work revolves around a central **purpose** or reason for existing. All work is conducted somewhere, in some **place**, whether it's on the 28th floor of a city sky-scraper or on a cruise ship in the middle of an ocean. All work requires a certain **time** commitment and is performed using various types of **tools**. **People** also play an important part in most jobs—whether the job involves interacting with lots or very few of them. And, especially from where you are sitting as a kid still in school, all work involves some type of **preparation** to learn how to do the job.

Another word for these six common ingredients is *values*. Each one represents important aspects of work that people value in different ways. The following activity will give you a chance to think about what matters most to you in each of these areas. That way you'll get a better idea of things to look for as you explore different careers.

Here's how the process works:

First, read the statements listed for each value on the fol-lowing pages. Decide which, if any, represent your idea of an ideal job.

Next, take a look at the grid on page 16. For every value statement with which you agreed, draw its symbol in the appropriate space on your grid. (If this book doesn't belong to you, use a blank sheet of paper to draw your own grid with six big spaces.) Or, if you want to get really fancy, cut pic-tures out of magazines and glue them into the appropriate space. If you do not see a symbol that represents your best answer, make up a new one and sketch it in the appropriate box.

When you are finished, you'll have a very useful picture of the kinds of values that matter most to you in your future job.

PURPOSE

Which of the following statements describes what you most hope to accomplish in your future work? Pick as many as are true for you and feel free to add others.

♥	❏	I want to help other people.
	❏	I want to make lots of money.
★	❏	I want to do something I really believe in.
	❏	I want to make things.
	❏	I want to use my brain power in challenging ways.
	❏	I want to work with my own creative ideas.
	❏	I want to be very successful.
	❏	I want to find a good company and stick with it for the rest of my life.
	❏	I want to be famous.

Other purpose-related things that are especially important to me are

PLACE

When you think about your future work, what kind of place would you most like to do it in? Pick as many as are true for you and feel free to add others.

	❏	I want to work in a big city skyscraper.
	❏	I want to work in a shopping mall or retail store.
	❏	I want to work in the great outdoors.
	❏	I want to travel a lot for my work.
	❏	I want to work out of my own home.
	❏	I want to work for a government agency.
	❏	I want to work in a school or university.
	❏	I want to work in a factory or laboratory.

Other place-related things that are especially important to me are

TIME

When you think about your future work, what kind of schedule sounds most appealing to you? Pick as many as are true for you and feel free to add others.

	❑	I'd rather work regular business hours—nine to five, Monday through Friday.
	❑	I'd like to have lots of vacation time.
	❑	I'd prefer a flexible schedule so I can balance my work, family, and personal needs.
	❑	I'd like to work nights only so my days are free.
	❑	I'd like to work where the pace is fast and I stay busy all day.
	❑	I'd like to work where I would always know exactly what I'm supposed to do.
	❑	I'd like to work where I could plan my own day.
	❑	I'd like to work where there's lots of variety and no two days are alike.

Other time-related things that are especially important to me are

TOOLS What kinds of things would you most like to work with? Pick as many as are true for you and feel free to add others.		
	❏	I'd prefer to work mostly with people.
	❏	I'd prefer to work mostly with technology.
	❏	I'd prefer to work mostly with machines.
	❏	I'd prefer to work mostly with products people buy.
	❏	I'd prefer to work mostly with planes, trains, automobiles, or other things that go.
	❏	I'd prefer to work mostly with ideas.
	❏	I'd prefer to work mostly with information.
	❏	I'd prefer to work mostly with nature.

Other tool-related things that are especially important to me are

PEOPLE		
What role do other people play in your future work? How many do you want to interact with on a daily basis? What age group would you most enjoy working with? Pick as many as are true for you and feel free to add others.		
	❑	I'd like to work with lots of people all day long.
	❑	I'd prefer to work alone most of the time.
	❑	I'd like to work as part of a team.
	❑	I'd like to work with people I might choose as friends.
	❑	I'd like to work with babies, children, or teenagers,
	❑	I'd like to work mostly with elderly people.
	❑	I'd like to work mostly with people who are in trouble.
	❑	I'd like to work mostly with people who are ill.
Other people-related things that are especially important to me are		

PREPARATION

When you think about your future work, how much time and energy do you want to devote to preparing for it? Pick as many as are true for you and feel free to add others.

	❏	I want to find a job that requires a college degree.
	❏	I want to find a job where I could learn what I need to know on the job.
	❏	I want to find a job that requires no additional training after I graduate from high school.
	❏	I want to find a job where the more education I get, the better my chances for a better job.
BOSS	❏	I want to run my own business and be my own boss.

Other preparation-related things that are especially important to me are

Now that you've uncovered some word clues about the types of values that are most important to you, use the grid on the following page (or use a separate sheet of paper if this book does not belong to you) to "paint a picture" of your ideal future career. Use the icons as ideas for how to visualize each statement. Or, if you'd like to get really creative, get a large sheet of paper, some markers, magazines, and glue or tape and create a collage.

PURPOSE	PLACE	TIME
TOOLS	**PEOPLE**	**PREPARATION**

DISCOVER #3: DANGEROUS DETOURS

Half of figuring out what you do want to do is figuring out what you don't want to do. Get a jump start on this process by making a list of 10 careers you already know you absolutely don't want to do.

Warning: Failure to heed early warnings signs to avoid careers like this can result in long hours of boredom and frustration spent doing a job you just weren't meant to do.

(If this book does not belong to you, make your list on a separate sheet of paper.)

1. _____   _____
2. _____   _____
3. _____   _____

4. _____   _____

5. _____   _____

6. _____   _____

7. _____   _____

8. _____   _____

9. _____   _____

10. _____   _____

Red Flag Summary:
Look over your list, and in the second column above (or on a separate sheet of paper) see if you can summarize what it is about these jobs that makes you want to avoid them like a bad case of cooties.

DISCOVER #4: ULTIMATE CAREER DESTINATION

Imagine that your dream job is like a favorite tourist destination, and you have to convince other people to pick it over every other career in the world. How would you describe it? What features make it especially appealing to you? What does a person have to do to have a career like it?

Take a blank sheet of paper and fold it into thirds. Fill each column on both sides with words and pictures that create a vivid image of what you'd most like your future career to be.

Special note: Just for now, instead of actually naming a specific career, describe what your ideal career would be like. In places where the name of the career would be used, leave a blank space like this _____. For instance: For people who want to become rich and famous, being a _____ is the way to go.

DISCOVER #5: GET SOME DIRECTION

It's easy to get lost when you don't have a good idea of where you want to go. This is especially true when you start thinking about what to do with the rest of your life. Unless you focus on where you want to go, you might get lost or even miss the exit. This discover exercise will help you connect your own interests and abilities with a whole world of career opportunities.

Mark the activities that you enjoy doing or would enjoy doing if you had the chance. Be picky. Don't mark ideas that you wish you would do. Mark only those that you would really do. For instance, if skydiving sounds appealing but you'd never do it because you are terrified of heights, don't mark it.

Please Note: If this book does not belong to you, write your responses on a separate sheet of paper.

❏ 1. Rescue a cat stuck in a tree
❏ 2. Paint a mural on the cafeteria wall
❏ 3. Run for student council
❏ 4. Send e-mail to a "pen pal" in another state
❏ 5. Find out all there is to know about the American Revolution
❏ 6. Survey your classmates to find out what they do after school
❏ 7. Try out for the school play
❏ 8. Dissect a frog and identify the different organs
❏ 9. Play baseball, soccer, football, or _____ (fill in your favorite sport)

❏ 10. Talk on the phone to just about anyone who will talk back

❏ 11. Try foods from all over the world—Thailand, Poland, Japan, etc.

❏ 12. Write poems about things that are happening in your life

❏ 13. Create a really scary haunted house to take your friends through on Halloween

❏ 14. Bake a cake and decorate it for your best friend's birthday

❏ 15. Sell enough advertisements for the school yearbook to win a trip to Walt Disney World

❏ 16. Simulate an imaginary flight through space on your computer screen

❏ 17. Collect stamps, coins, baseball cards, or whatever and organize them into a fancy display

❏ 18. Build model airplanes, boats, doll houses, or anything from kits

❏ 19. Teach your friends a new dance routine

❏ 20. Watch the stars come out at night and see how many constellations you can find

❏ 21. Watch baseball, soccer, football, or _____ (fill in your favorite sport) on TV

❏ 22. Give a speech in front of the entire school

❏ 23. Plan the class field trip to Washington, D.C.

❏ 24 Read everything in sight, including the back of the cereal box

❏ 25. Figure out "who dunnit" in a mystery story

❏ 26. Make a poster announcing the school football game

❏ 27. Think up a new way to make the lunch line move faster and explain it to the cafeteria staff

❏ 28. Put together a multimedia show for a school assembly using music and lots of pictures and graphics

❏ 29. Visit historic landmarks like the Statue of Liberty and Civil War battlegrounds

❏ 30. Invest your allowance in the stock market and keep track of how it does

GET IN GEAR!

- ❏ 31. Go to the ballet or opera every time you get the chance
- ❏ 32. Do experiments with a chemistry set
- ❏ 33. Keep score at your sister's Little League game
- ❏ 34. Use lots of funny voices when reading stories to children
- ❏ 35. Ride on airplanes, trains, boats—anything that moves
- ❏ 36. Interview the new exchange student for an article in the school newspaper
- ❏ 37. Build your own treehouse
- ❏ 38. Visit an art museum and pick out your favorite painting
- ❏ 39. Play Monopoly in an all-night championship challenge
- ❏ 40. Make a chart on the computer to show how much soda students buy from the school vending machines each week
- ❏ 41. Find out all you can about your family ancestors and make a family tree
- ❏ 42. Keep track of how much your team earns to buy new uniforms
- ❏ 43. Play an instrument in the school band or orchestra
- ❏ 44. Take things apart and put them back together again
- ❏ 45. Write stories about sports for the school newspaper

❏ 46. Listen to other people talk about their problems
❏ 47. Imagine yourself in exotic places
❏ 48. Hang around bookstores and libraries
❏ 49. Play harmless practical jokes on April Fools' Day
❏ 50. Take photographs at the school talent show
❏ 51. Make money by setting up your own business—
     paper route, lemonade stand, etc.
❏ 52. Create an imaginary city using a computer
❏ 53. Look for Native American artifacts and arrowheads
❏ 54. Do 3-D puzzles
❏ 55. Keep track of the top 10 songs of the week
❏ 56. Read about famous inventors and their inventions
❏ 57. Make play-by-play announcements at the school
     football game
❏ 58. Answer the phones during a telethon to raise
     money for orphans
❏ 59. Be an exchange student in another country
❏ 60. Write down all your secret thoughts and favorite
     sayings in a journal
❏ 61. Jump out of an airplane (with a parachute, of course)
❏ 62. Use a video camera to make your own movies
❏ 63. Get your friends together to help clean up your
     town after a hurricane

❏ 64. Spend your summer at a computer camp learning lots of new computer programs

❏ 65. Help your little brother or sister make ink out of blueberry juice

❏ 66. Build bridges, skyscrapers, and other structures out of LEGOs

❏ 67. Plan a concert in the park for little kids

❏ 68. Collect different kinds of rocks

❏ 69. Help plan a sports tournament

❏ 70. Be DJ for the school dance

❏ 71. Learn how to fly a plane or sail a boat

❏ 72. Write funny captions for pictures in the school yearbook

❏ 73. Scuba dive to search for buried treasure

❏ 74. Sketch pictures of your friends

❏ 75. Pick out neat stuff to sell at the school store

❏ 76. Answer your classmates' questions about how to use the computer

❏ 77. Make a timeline showing important things that happened during the year

❏ 78. Draw a map showing how to get to your house from school

❏ 79. Make up new words to your favorite songs

❏ 80. Take a hike and name the different kinds of trees, birds, or flowers

❏ 81. Referee intramural basketball games

❏ 82. Join the school debate team

❏ 83. Make a poster with postcards from all the places you went on your summer vacation

❏ 84. Write down stories that your grandparents tell you about when they were young

CALCULATE THE CLUES

Now is your chance to add it all up. Each of the 12 boxes on the following pages contains an interest area that is common to both your world and the world of work. Follow these directions to discover your personal Skill Set:

1. Find all of the numbers that you checked on pages 18–23 in the following boxes and mark them

with an X. Work your way all the way through number 84.

2. Go back and count the Xs marked for each interest area. Write that number in the space that says "Total."

3. Find the interest area with the highest total and put a number one in the "Rank" blank of that box. Repeat this process for the next two highest scoring areas. Rank the second highest as number two and the third highest as number three.

4. If you have more than three strong areas, choose the three that are most important and interesting to you.

Remember: If this book does not belong to you, write your responses on a separate sheet of paper.

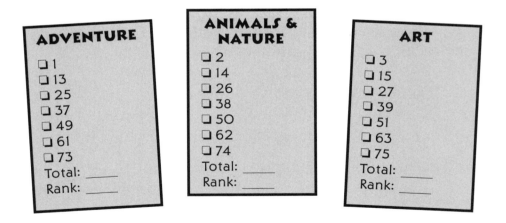

ADVENTURE
- ❑ 1
- ❑ 13
- ❑ 25
- ❑ 37
- ❑ 49
- ❑ 61
- ❑ 73

Total: _____
Rank: _____

ANIMALS & NATURE
- ❑ 2
- ❑ 14
- ❑ 26
- ❑ 38
- ❑ 50
- ❑ 62
- ❑ 74

Total: _____
Rank: _____

ART
- ❑ 3
- ❑ 15
- ❑ 27
- ❑ 39
- ❑ 51
- ❑ 63
- ❑ 75

Total: _____
Rank: _____

BUSINESS

- ❏ 4
- ❏ 16
- ❏ 28
- ❏ 40
- ❏ 52
- ❏ 64
- ❏ 76

Total: _____
Rank: _____

COMPUTERS

- ❏ 5
- ❏ 17
- ❏ 29
- ❏ 41
- ❏ 53
- ❏ 65
- ❏ 77

Total: _____
Rank: _____

MATH

- ❏ 6
- ❏ 18
- ❏ 30
- ❏ 42
- ❏ 54
- ❏ 66
- ❏ 78

Total: _____
Rank: _____

MUSIC/DANCE

- ❏ 7
- ❏ 19
- ❏ 31
- ❏ 43
- ❏ 55
- ❏ 67
- ❏ 79

Total: _____
Rank: _____

SCIENCE

- ❏ 8
- ❏ 20
- ❏ 32
- ❏ 44
- ❏ 56
- ❏ 68
- ❏ 80

Total: _____
Rank: _____

SPORTS

- ❏ 9
- ❏ 21
- ❏ 33
- ❏ 45
- ❏ 57
- ❏ 69
- ❏ 81

Total: _____
Rank: _____

TALKING

- ❏ 10
- ❏ 22
- ❏ 34
- ❏ 46
- ❏ 58
- ❏ 70
- ❏ 82

Total: _____
Rank: _____

TRAVEL

- ❏ 11
- ❏ 23
- ❏ 35
- ❏ 47
- ❏ 59
- ❏ 71
- ❏ 83

Total: _____
Rank: _____

WRITING

- ❏ 12
- ❏ 24
- ❏ 36
- ❏ 48
- ❏ 60
- ❏ 72
- ❏ 84

Total: _____
Rank: _____

What are your top three interest areas? List them here (or on a separate piece of paper).

1. _____

2. _____

3. _____

This is your personal Skill Set and provides important clues about the kinds of work you're most likely to enjoy. Remember it and look for career ideas with a Skill Set that matches yours most closely. You'll find a Skill Set box at the beginning of each career profile in the following section.

TAKE A TRIP!

Cruise down the career idea highway and enjoy in-depth profiles of some of the interesting options in this field. Keep in mind all that you've discovered about yourself so far. Find the careers that match your own Skill Set first. After that, keep on trucking through the other ideas—exploration is the name of this game.

If becoming a professional athlete is your dream and you've got the talent, then go for it with all you've got. But remember, playing sports is only one way to make a living in the multibillion dollar sports industry. Make sure that you also have a full understanding of all the exciting ways to build a career around sports. Even those who do make it to the pros need to have a plan for life after their playing days are over.

The sports industry in the United States employs more than 4 million people. Only a small percentage of this number represents players. That means there's plenty of opportunity for an amazing variety of sports-related career options. So, hold fast to your dreams and enjoy this look at some of the many ways to make sports a big part of your career.

Meanwhile, as you read about the following careers, imagine yourself doing each job and ask yourself the following questions:

☼ Would I like it?
☼ Would I be good at it?
☼ Is it the stuff my career dreams are made of?

If so, make a quick exit to explore what it involves, try it out, check it out, and get acquainted! Look out for the symbols below.

Buckle up and enjoy the trip!

☞ TRY IT OUT

✔ CHECK IT OUT

🖱 ON THE WEB

📚 AT THE LIBRARY

🗣 WITH THE EXPERTS

A NOTE ON WEB SITES

Internet sites tend to move around the Web a bit. If you have trouble finding a particular site, use an Internet browser to find a specific Web site or type of information.

Agent

WHAT IS AN AGENT?

Technically speaking, a sports agent is anyone who finds a good athlete, signs him or her as a client, and gets him or her a job with a professional sports team. Sometimes an athlete will ask a parent or trusted friend to serve as their official representative; however, the best (and most highly paid) agents tend to come from a business, accounting, or law background, and they often have strong ties to a particular sport. They represent a number of clients and are recognized as "official" agents by one or more of the professional sports organizations (NFL, NBA, etc.). Most important, they have earned a reputation for providing ethical and professional services for their athletic clients.

An agent's job is to negotiate the best possible contract for his or her clients. An agent serves as the go-between (and quite often, the voice of reason) between an athlete and the sports club. Sports agents must keep their client's best interests at heart while they work out the financial and legal details of a player's position with the team. In return, they receive a cut (usually between 5 and 20 percent) of the player's salary.

An agent's job isn't finished after a client is signed to a major team. An agent also looks for opportunities for clients to endorse products, appear in commercials, and make personal appearances. These sometimes lucrative opportunities can involve almost any product, from athletic equipment and clothes to hamburgers and soft drinks. An agent may also look for ways to involve a client in charitable causes and events. Sometimes agents also help their clients manage their finances and handle other personal matters so that the clients can concentrate on what they do best: sports.

Law, business, or accounting provide the necessary educational background to become an agent. To get on-the-job experience, aspiring agents would do well to start their careers in a sports management agency, a sports arena complex, a professional sports club, or any other place that involves working in the middle of all the sports action. Typical of any career where the financial stakes are high and the potential to earn big bucks is great, this is a very competitive profession. It takes a good business mind, a real love of sports, an ability to earn and

keep the trust of clients, and a lot of hard work to find success as a sports agent.

 **TRY IT OUT**

NEGOTIATE THE BIG ONE

It is safe to assume that the number-one financial issue fac-
ing most people your age is their allowance. Can you get by
on your current "salary"? Think about it and look for ways to
build a case for a raise. Have you recently taken on more
household chores? Maybe because of extracurricular activities you have more expenses like taking public transporta-
tion or buying a snack to tide you over until dinner time.
Come up with a written plan for negotiating an increase in
your allowance. Keep in mind the universal WIIFM (what's in
it for me) aspect of every deal and consider your parents'
perspective. What can you offer them in return for a raise?
Pick a good time to bring up the subject (such as when your
room is clean and all your chores are done) and pitch your
plan. Next thing you know you'll have to decide how to spend
all that extra money.

DRUMMING UP BUSINESS

Most agents actively seek their clients, rather than waiting
for them to walk through their door. To snag the best clients, they have to keep track of new talent and be ready to
approach them before the big offers start pouring in.

Get a head start on your career as a sports agent by learning how to spot tomorrow's superstars before they make
it to the top. First, pick your favorite sport. Start following
news coverage of high school and college players who seem
to show exceptional athletic abilities. Make notes and keep
news clippings about those you think might make it to the
next level of being recruited for a good college or pro team.
Keep tabs on their progress. Follow along for more than one
season and see if your hunches are right.

✓ CHECK IT OUT

🖱 ON THE WEB
ONLINE SPORTS
Catch all the sports action online at these Web sites:

- ⚲ Catch the latest news from Sports Illustrated for Kids at http://www.sikids.com.
- ⚲ Find links to all kinds of sports Web sites at http://www.northvalley.net/kids/sports.shtml.
- ⚲ Find even more links to sports stuff online at http://cybersleuth-kids.com/sleuth/Sports.
- ⚲ Another big sports site with lots of links can be found at http://school.discovery.com/schrockguide/popspt.html.

LET'S MAKE A DEAL
Negotiation, conflict resolution, fighting fair—it's all in a day's work for sports agents. Find out how to go for the win-win in every situation with strategies found at the following Web sites:

- ⚲ View *Out on a Limb: A Guide to Getting Along* at http://www.urbanext.uiuc.edu/conflict/index.html.
- ⚲ Learn five steps to solving problems peacefully at http://www.annies.com/kids/peaceful_conflict_resolution.html.
- ⚲ Find out how some kids are getting serious about sowing seeds of peace around the world at http://www.seedsofpeace.org/site/PageServer.
- ⚲ Goof around with some of the world's best nego-tiators at the Nobel Peace Prize game Web site at http://nobelprize.org/peace/educational/index.html.
- ⚲ Learn how to deal with bullies at http://pbskids.org/itsmylife/friends/bullies.

AT THE LIBRARY

GET YOUR ACT TOGETHER

Most sports agents would agree that it's a lot easier to manage someone else's life or career if you know how to manage your own. Get your act together by following some of the advice found in books such as:

Carlson, Richard. *Don't Sweat the Small Stuff for Teens: Simple Ways to Keep Your Cool in Stressful Times.* New York: Hyperion, 2000.

Covey, Sean. *7 Habits of Highly Effective Teens.* New York: Simon and Schuster, 1998.

Fox, Janet. *Get Organized Without Losing It.* Minneapolis: Free Spirit, 2006.

Johnson, Spencer. *Who Moved My Cheese for Teens.* New York: Penguin, 2002.

McGraw, Jay. *Life Strategies for Teens.* New York: Simon and Schuster, 2000.

SUB AT THE TOP OF YOUR GAME

Daydream just a little bit and try to imagine what it would be like to represent clients such as these star athletes:

Berstein, Ross. *Amazing Athletes: Shaquille O'Neal.* Minneapolis: Lerner, 2004.

Doeden, Matt. *Amazing Athletes: Shaun White.* Minneapolis: Lerner, 2007.

Donovan, Sandy. *Amazing Athletes: Derek Jeter.* Minneapolis: Lerner, 2004.

———. *Amazing Athletes: Lance Armstrong.* Minneapolis: Lerner, 2006.

Savage, Jeff. *Amazing Athletes: Danica Patrick.* Minneapolis: Lerner, 2007.

———. *Amazing Athletes: LeBron James.* Minneapolis: Lerner, 2006.

———. *Amazing Athletes: Peyton Manning.* Minneapolis: Lerner, 2006.

————. *Amazing Athletes: Sammy Sosa.* Minneapolis: Lerner, 2005.

————. *Amazing Athletes: Tiger Woods.* Minneapolis: Lerner, 2007.

————. *Amazing Athletes: Yao Ming.* Minneapolis: Lerner, 2004.

WITH THE EXPERTS

Black Sports Agents Association (BSAA)
9255 Sunset Boulevard. Suite 1120
Beverly Hills, CA 90069
http://www.blacksportsagents.com

North American Society for Sports Management (NASSM)
West Gym 014
Slippery Rock University
Slippery Rock, PA 16057
http://www.nassm.com

National Sports Law Institute
1103 West Wisconsin Avenue
Milwaukee, WI 53201-2313
http://law.marquette.edu/cgi–bin/site.pl?2130&pageID=160

GET ACQUAINTED

Richard DeLuca, Sports Agent

CAREER PATH

CHILDHOOD ASPIRATION: To be a baseball or football player.

FIRST JOB: Working in a sporting goods store.

CURRENT JOB: President of Integrated Sports Management.

THE RIGHT PLACE AT THE RIGHT TIME

Sports have been part of Richard DeLuca's life from the time he was a child. In high school he focused on three sports: tennis, basketball, and soccer. At Tulane University, it turned out that his best connection to sports were his two athletic dorm mates. When they were offered contracts to play professional sports and were uncertain about a shady agent that wanted to handle the deal, they turned to DeLuca. They figured that since DeLuca was headed to law school he would know what to do.

DeLuca helped out his friends and simultaneously set the course for his career. He contacted a reputable sports agent and explained the situation. The agent said that if DeLuca could bring these new players to his firm, he would give DeLuca a job. That's how DeLuca wound up spending his first two years at law school at the University of Miami learning how to be a sports agent. When the agency wound up representing two first-round draft picks, things got so crazy at work that DeLuca left law school to devote all his time to his work.

Looking back, DeLuca credits three things for getting him where he is today: friendship, geography (the University of Miami had a number of top players back then), and his own desire to intermingle a career with sports and law.

MAKING IT WORK

Several years ago, DeLuca went out on his own and started a new agency. Knowing that he'd have to bring something substantial to the market in order to compete with other agents, he developed a full-service approach to player management. He had already learned that managing an athlete's finances was completely the opposite of managing the finances of other professionals. Instead of starting out with low earnings and building to higher earnings over several decades, professional athletes start out with big earnings that drop drastically in only a few years. DeLuca recognized that most athletes have just one shot at setting themselves up financially. He had witnessed far too many situations in which the athletes make money early but then blow it, leaving them nothing when they retire.

DeLuca starts at the very beginning by identifying college football players with the potential to make it in the pros. Once his agency signs a player, the real work begins on two levels. One level involves aggressively "selling" the player to all the NFL teams with a well-orchestrated promotional blitz. On the other levels, DeLuca's firm works with the players to get them ready to survive in the business world. Sometimes this involves things as basic as teaching players how to balance a checkbook. Then the firm helps get the players established by setting up a bank account, securing a line of credit, and educating them about how to handle their finances.

Once an offer has been made and the all-important contract negotiated, more of DeLuca's full-service commitment comes into play. DeLuca's partner Tom Jacobs is an accountant, so he handles the financial side of things such as investments, taxes, and money management. DeLuca, meanwhile, makes it a point to touch base with every client at least once a week and travels to see each client play at least once a year. Some players feel as though DeLuca is part of the family.

FINDING A NICHE

DeLuca is keenly aware of the tough competition his firm faces in the sports industry. Through the years, he's learned to combat the situation by distinguishing his agency from the rest of the pack in unique ways. Certainly his reputation for taking good care of players and the full-service approach to player management are key to his success. Another point that sets his agency apart is that he and his partner focus on representing players from smaller colleges—schools that other agents tend to ignore.

The approach has obviously paid off since DeLuca's agency is one of the largest in the South and among the top 25 in the entire country. Representing players such as Brad Maynard and Jason McKie of the Chicago Bears, C.C. Brown of the Houston Texans, Maurice Hicks of the San Francisco 49ers, and Derek Miller of the Oakland Raiders, DeLuca has established himself as an agent to be trusted by players and reckoned with by other agents.

A DOSE OF REALITY

When young people ask him for advice about becoming a sports agent, DeLuca tells them, "don't do it." Of course he knows that for some people the pull of the profession is so great that there is no way that they won't do it. But he also knows the odds. For instance, while there are approximately 2,000 football players in the United States, there are about 1,500 agents (officially certified and otherwise). Since 10 of the biggest sports management firms represent about 500 players, that leaves 700 players for the rest.

If trying this profession is something you can't resist, DeLuca recommends starting with an established firm. He says that getting the first client is the toughest part. Get one, do a good job, and others will follow.

Athlete

SKILL SET

✔ ADVENTURE

✔ TRAVEL

✔ SPORTS

WHAT IS AN ATHLETE?

Just about anyone with a serious interest in sports has entertained thoughts of becoming a professional athlete. For some, it's a passing fancy. For others, it's a dream to be relentlessly pursued.

If you have hopes of someday becoming a great sports figure, the first thing you need to do is take a realistic look at what it requires. Media hype surrounding multimillion-dollar contracts and all the televised excitement of big game days may make the sports profession appear a bit rosier than it is for most people. Granted, sports can be an interesting and even glamorous way to make a living, but the reality is that it's not all fun and games. Before you set your heart on a career as a professional athlete, weigh the costs as described in the following "reality checks."

Reality check #1: Are you *exceptionally* good at your chosen sport? Notice the emphasis on the word "exceptionally." You may be the best player on your team or in your town, but do you have the talent to compete in a profession where there is fierce competition for each and every spot on each and every team? There's always going to be someone bigger and better than you. If you're going to make it in the pros, you have to distinguish yourself from the rest of the pack and show remarkable skill and staying power. Quite often, at least part of an athlete's success can be attributed to natural talent—you either have it or you don't. Other times success is as much a result of hard work and determination as it is of ability.

Reality check #2: Are you willing to do whatever it takes to play your sport? There are some pretty high costs associated with playing sports professionally. Many of these costs can be summarized in one word: commitment. Playing at the top of any game requires a commitment to practice, practice, practice. That often means getting up earlier than everyone else and sticking with it when everyone else has gone home. It often means choosing practice over goofing off with friends, getting a part-time job, and other fun activities that are a normal part of a typical teenager's life. Commitment to the game doesn't start when you are on the payroll for a pro team. It starts right now and continues throughout your career. It boils down to choosing sports as the number-one priority in your life. Perhaps more than anything else, this decision to commit separates the wishful thinkers from those who have what it takes to go all the way.

Reality check #3: Do you want to play sports badly enough to sacrifice physical and personal comforts? It's almost inevitable that somewhere along the line a professional athlete is going to take a hard knock or two. Many athletes find that physical pain becomes a constant companion. Think about whether or not you want to risk your physical well-being for the sake of your sport.

When it comes to personal comforts, you'll also need to think about how you'd like spending a majority (or at least a good portion) of your time on the road. On one hand, a career in sports can be a great way to see the world. On the other hand, it can get lonely and boring being away from home, family, and friends so much of the time.

Reality check #4: Are you willing to start at the bottom and work your way up to the top? First, you'll have to prove yourself on the high school level so that a good college will pick you for the team. Then you'll have to prove yourself on the college level so that a pro team will even consider looking at you. Even after you've been signed to the big time, you may spend a lot of time playing for minor leagues or warming a bench waiting until you're ready to compete with the pros.

These are some real issues that you'll have to face if you're going to make it in this competitive profession. If you've thought through all these reality checks and are still game for a shot at the pros, here's what you need to do to move closer to making your dream come true.

Obviously, the first thing you need to do is play your sport whenever you can. Try out for the team and work hard to improve your skills. Record your progress on videotape. Once you play well enough, you can use some of the best action shots to put together a video résumé to send to coaches at colleges with notable sports programs. Ask your coach to help you choose colleges that match your abilities and aspirations. At the same time, make sure that sports isn't the only thing you work at while you are in school. Good grades are key to making and staying on any athletic team; if you flunk your courses, you're off the team.

Give yourself a chance at a lifetime of success and get a great education. Even in a best-case scenario in which you make it to the pinnacle of your sport, your career as an athlete will sustain you for only a dozen years or so. Be prepared to tackle the rest of your life with the gusto you brought to sports.

# TRY IT OUT

LEAVE NO STONE UNTURNED

Everyone knows about the big three sports—baseball, football, and basketball—which means there's more competition to play these sports. Soccer and hockey are two increasingly popular sports with professional and semiprofessional playing opportunities. If you are convinced you want to pursue a career as an athlete, one of these sports may be just the ticket. Also, don't overlook opportunities to compete in some of the following sports:

automobile racing	ice skating	synchronized swimming
bodybuilding	lacrosse	tennis
bowling	racquetball	triathlon
golf	rodeo	waterskiing
gymnastics	skiing	weightlifting
horse racing	surfing	yachting

Pick one that sounds interesting to you, use your favorite Internet search engine (such as http://www.google.com or http://www.yahoo.com) to find information about it, and use what you learn to create a poster to recruit young athletes into the sport.

KEEP YOUR EYES ON THE STARS

Every person who has ever excelled in sports started out just like you—with a hope and a dream. You can learn from other athletes' successes and failures. Pick a favorite sports hero or two. Start collecting all the information you can about his or her career and early background. You can find information in books, magazines, and newspapers. You can also use an Internet web browser such as Yahoo! or Explorer to find information on the World Wide Web. Compile everything you find in a notebook and keep tabs on your hero's career.

RAINY DAY SPORTS
Even the most dedicated sports players have to go home sometime. But, thanks to computer technology, the game doesn't have to stop. For nonstop action and some subtle athletic training tips, use your computer to play simulated sports games. You'll find quite a variety of options anywhere software is sold.

SHAPE UP!
Peak performance in any sport demands that an athlete be in top physical condition. Staying in good condition demands that you establish and maintain healthy habits in fitness and nutrition. Ask your physical education teacher or your coach to help draw up a plan for getting and staying in shape. Consider both nutrition and exercise. Make a chart to record your progress for a few weeks until these healthy habits become a part of your everyday lifestyle. For ideas and inspiration go online to http://www.verbnow.com.

✔ CHECK IT OUT

ON THE WEB
DREAM TEAMS
Pick a favorite sport and pick a favorite team, then go online to learn more about your favorite players.

- Major League Baseball (MLB) at http://mlb.mlb.com/index.jsp
- National Basketball League (NBA) at http://www.nba.com
- National Football League (NFL) at http://www.nfl.com
- U.S. Soccer Federation at http://www.ussoccer.com
- National Hockey League (NHL) at http://www.nhl.com
- National Lacrosse League (NLL) at http://www.nll.com

☀ Professional Golf Association (PGA) at http://www
.pga.com

If your top sport is not listed here, use an Internet browser
to look for it.
Also check out these online resources:

☀ Play games and test your trivia prowess at NFL Play
Football at http://www.playfootball.com/games.
☀ Find links to several fun baseball games at http://
resources.kaboose.com/games/baseball.html.
☀ It's b-ball time at http://www.nbaballers.com.
☀ Get in the games at the Sports Illustrated for Kids
Web site at http://sikids.com/games.
☀ Put together your own baseball, basketball, football,
or hockey dream teams at http://sikids.com/fantasy.

AT THE LIBRARY

HEADLINE SPORTS

Find out more about your favorite sports and athletic heroes
in books such as:

Buckley, Jim. *NBA: On the Inside*. New York: Scholastic, 2003.
———. *Recordbreakers*. New York: Scholastic, 2003.
Mason, Paul. *Training for the Top: Nutrition and Exercise*.
Chicago: Raintree, 2005.
McDaniels, Pellom. *So You Want to be a Pro*. Shawnee Mission,
Kan.: Addax, 2002.
Packard, Mary. *Beating the Odds*. New York: Children's Press, 2004.
Rappoport, Ken. *Ladies First: Women Athletes Who Made A
Difference*. Atlanta, Ga.: Peachtree, 2005.
———. *Profiles in Sports Courage*. Atlanta, Ga.: Peachtree, 2006.
Roberts, Robin. *Sports Injuries*. Minneapolis: Millbrook Press,
2001.
Streissguth, Thomas. *Jesse Owens*. Minneapolis: Lerner Publica-
tions, 2005.
Teitelbaum, Michael. *Great Moments in Women's Sports*. New
York: World Almanac, 2002.

 **WITH THE EXPERTS**

Amateur Athletic Union of the United States
PO Box 22409
Lake Buena Vista, FL 32830-2409
http://aausports.org

Athletes in Action
651 Taylor Drive
Xenia, OH 45385-7246
http://www.aia.com

Federation of Professional Athletes
2021 L Street, NW
Washington, DC 20036-4909

National Sports Foundation
PO Box 888886
Atlanta, GA 30356-0886
http://www.natlsportsfoundation.com

North American Youth Sports Institute
4985 Oak Garden Drive
Kernersville, NC 27284-9520
http://www.naysi.com

GET ACQUAINTED

Lionel Washington,
Professional Athlete

CAREER PATH

CHILDHOOD ASPIRATION:
To be a construction worker like
his dad.

FIRST JOB: Worked at a summer camp for children.

CURRENT JOB: Green Bay
Packers coach; former linebacker
for the Los Angeles Raiders.

A NATURAL FIT

Lionel Washington first played football when he was 11 or 12 years old. He thought it was a fun game, but he played mostly because his friends were playing. He didn't play football again until he was in high school; instead he played basketball throughout junior high. Washington lettered in football, basketball, and track in high school, and it was about then that Washington started wondering if he just might be blessed with some natural athletic talent. Learning new sports came easy to him.

Playing the new sports well was another story. Washington was always keenly aware that there would always be someone out there who was better than he was. Knowing this motivated him to work extra hard. Even as a teenager, Washington set goals for himself and didn't let anyone stop him from reaching them.

All this hard work paid off when he received scholarship offers from colleges all over the country. He choose to stay close to his Louisiana home and went to Tulane University, where he majored in sports administration and physical education.

SOMETHING'S UP

Washington continued to excel at football at Tulane, but he also recognized that getting a good education was key to his future success. The academic part of college was very hard for him at first because he hadn't learned good study habits. He knuckled down and applied the same hard work principles that he used on the football field to his homework and was able to graduate in four years.

Ever since the summer he'd spent working at a camp, Washington had wanted to work with children, and he had every intention of graduating and getting a job as a coach. The NFL had other plans for Washington.

He was picked up by the St. Louis Cardinals in the fourth round of the 1983 NFL draft. He played with the Cardinals for four years until he was traded to the Los Angeles Raiders. As of the 1998 season, he'd been playing professional football for 15 years and held the record for playing the position of cornerback longer than any other professional in history. It's a tough position that requires as much mental strength as it does physical prowess.

MORE THAN MEETS THE EYE

Washington says that it's hard for most people to imagine how demanding it is to play professional football. The Sunday games are so exciting that it's easy to glamorize and over-simplify the situation. In reality, the players put in a lot of work between games. He discovered that using brain power is just as important as brawn when it comes to preparing for a game. Players have to review game films, read up on their opponents, and memorize complicated game plans. These guys have to stay on top of the game intellectually, and they are smarter than they are often given credit for.

FOOTBALL CAREER, PART TWO

After 15 years as a professional football player, Washington was ready for a new challenge (and his body was definitely ready for a break!). But what does a defensive back with more years experience in his position than any other player in the NFL and an impressive 37 career interceptions do for an encore? He puts all that experience to good use coaching defensive cornerbacks, that's what.

In Washington's case, he joined the Green Bay Packers' coaching staff in 1999 and, since then, has been credited with impacting an impressive roster of defensive players. For instance, one of his star players, Al Harris, has been named the NFL's top-ranked passing defense with 18 pass defenses and three interceptions to his credit. As it turns out, Washington is a natural teacher. Under his tutelage in 2005, no other defense in the league allowed fewer passing yards per game (167.5) or passing first downs (143).

ADVICE TO ASPIRING ATHLETES

One word sums it up best: learn! Washington says that if you master the basics like reading and study skills, you won't have to struggle as hard to do whatever it is you want to do. Learn how to learn, and you can defeat any obstacle.

Also, don't put all your eggs in one basket. Washington urges anyone with a desire to become a professional athlete to prepare for it and pursue it with all you've got. Just don't let it keep you from considering other options.

Athletic Trainer

SKILL SET

✔ ADVENTURE

✔ SPORTS

✔ TALKING

GO enroll in an American Red Cross first aid course.

READ the sports pages of the newspaper to follow who's on the injured list and what's being done to help get them back in the game.

TRY naming all the bones in the human leg. Use pictures in an anatomy book to teach yourself.

WHAT IS A TRAINER?

Wherever there are people playing sports, there are people getting hurt. A look at annual statistics indicates that millions of people get hurt every year playing everything from bowling to soccer to wrestling. In many cases, especially in organized sports programs, an athletic trainer is the first person on the scene to evaluate and begin treating sports-related injuries. Cool, calm, and collected are words that describe the best athletic trainers in these types of crisis situations.

Along with providing on-the-scene assistance to injured players, athletic trainers are also involved in important ways before and after injuries occur. The top priority of every athletic trainer is to prevent injuries from ever happening. They do this by making sure that the athletes are in peak physical condition, that they are getting the strengthening and conditioning exercises they need, and that their diets support the special demands their profession puts on their bodies.

Athletic trainers also have important responsibilities after someone is injured. For one thing, an athletic trainer may act as a liaison between the athlete and the medical professionals who treat the injuries. It is often up to the athletic trainer to help an athlete understand the nature of the injury and offer guidance in making important decisions about the best medical options. Sometimes, it means being on hand to provide support and encouragement during painful surgeries and other treatments. After the medical professionals do all they can, an athletic trainer steps in to help get the athlete back in the game. This process may involve special physical therapy sessions, heat, whirlpool, or massage treatments.

While it is ultimately up to the player to decide when to return to the game, most players count on unbiased recommendations from the team doctor and athletic trainer about when the time is right. Ultimately, it is up to the athletic trainer to decide when and if a player is ready to play. One of the biggest ethical dilemmas a trainer may face is keeping players off the roster until their bodies are completely healed in spite of intense pressure to get them back in action. With some players being crucial to the game, some athletic trainers might be tempted to rush the rehabilitation process.

Athletic trainers are employed in high schools, colleges, universities, and professional sports teams. Most athletic trainers at the high school level also teach or coach at least part time. Other athletic trainers work in sports centers or clinics helping treat the 18 million or so people who are injured each year playing sports. With more than $10 billion being spent on rehabilitation programs alone (not including surgery, treatment, and prevention), there is plenty of opportunity for well-trained and committed sports medicine professionals.

To become an officially recognized athletic trainer, you must be certified by the National Athletic Trainers Association. This requires earning a college degree in a field such as physical education, kinesiology (the study of body movement and anatomy), coaching, or sports medicine as well as meeting some very specific internship requirements and passing some special tests. It helps if you start college with a pretty good idea that you want to become an athletic trainer so that you can complete the internship requirement while you earn your degree.

While athletic trainers might seem the most obvious job in sports medicine, there are other options you might want to consider, including physical therapist, nutritionist, or kinesiologist. In addition, many full-fledged medical doctors and dentists devote themselves to the practice of sports-related medicine.

☞ TRY IT OUT

FIRST AID KIT

When you get a bunch of people together running around, playing hard, swinging things, and chasing balls, someone will eventually get hurt. Make a chart with tips on how to handle common sports injuries such as cuts and scrapes, dislocations, heat exhaustion, nosebleeds, tooth loss, and concussion.

You'll find useful information in first-aid books at your local library or in Web sites such as:

- ☼ http://www.healthy.net/clinic/firstaid
- ☼ http://kidshealth.org/parent/firstaid_safe

☼ http://www.mayoclinic.com/health/FirstAidIndex/
FirstAidIndex

GET A HEAD START ON THE ACTION

Do you have what it takes to be an athletic trainer? Find out now by getting involved in your school or community recreation sports programs. Talk to the coach or athletic director to see where he or she needs the most help.

Before you get started, you'll have to learn some basics. You can do this by taking a first aid and perhaps even a CPR course through the American Red Cross (http://www.redcross .org).

✔ CHECK IT OUT

🖰 ON THE WEB

THE SPORTS DOCTOR IS IN

You've got a busy day of surgery putting busted up athletes back together again. First on your schedule is a knee surgery. Scrub in and get started at http://www.edheads .org/activities/knee/swf/surgery.htm.

Hip surgery is next on your schedule. Participate in an animated virtual hip surgery at http://www.edheads.org/ activities/hip/swf/index.htm.

PRE-MED ONLINE

Sports trainers have a background in medicine. Following are some fun Web sites where you can give your own medical training a jumpstart:

☼ Solve some medical mysteries at http://medmyst .rice.edu
☼ Stalk the mysterious microbe at http://www.microbe .org
☼ Explore your gross and cool body at http://yucky .kids.discovery.com/noflash/body/index.html

- Explore biology with the Howard Hughes Medical Center at http://www.hhmi.org/coolscience
- Take an interactive tour of cells, bacteria, and viruses at http://www.cellsalive.com

AT THE LIBRARY

AN OUNCE OF PREVENTION

Find out how to prevent, treat, and diagnose common sports injuries in the *Sports Injuries* series for young readers like you. Among the 17 titles in this interesting series are:

Lee, Veronica. *Field Hockey.* Broomhall, Pa.: Mason Crest, 2003.

McCoy, Lisa. *Cheerleading.* Broomhall, Pa.: Mason Crest, 2003.

McNab, Chris. *Extreme Sports.* Broomhall, Pa.: Mason Crest, 2003.

———. *Volleyball.* Broomhall, Pa.: Mason Crest, 2003.

Wright, John. *Baseball.* Broomhall, Pa.: Mason Crest, 2003.

———. *Basketball.* Broomhall, Pa.: Mason Crest, 2003.

———. *Football.* Broomhall, Pa.: Mason Crest, 2003.

WITH THE EXPERTS

American Medical Athletic Association
4405 East-West Highway, Suite 405
Bethesda, MD 20814-4535
http://www.amaasportsmed.org

International Center for Sports Nutrition
502 South 44th Street, Room 3007
Omaha, NE 68105-1065
http://www.sportsnutritionsociety.org

National Athletic Trainers Association
2952 Stemmons Freeway
Dallas, TX 75247-6113
http://www.nata.org

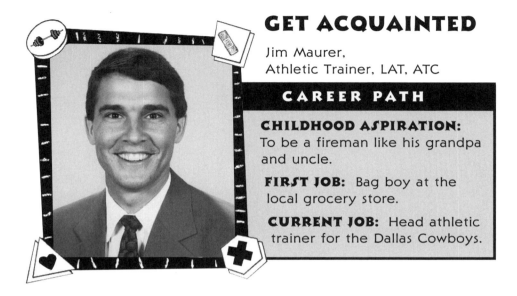

GET ACQUAINTED

Jim Maurer,
Athletic Trainer, LAT, ATC

CAREER PATH

CHILDHOOD ASPIRATION:
To be a fireman like his grandpa
and uncle.

FIRST JOB: Bag boy at the
local grocery store.

CURRENT JOB: Head athletic
trainer for the Dallas Cowboys.

A BIG BROTHER'S ADVICE

Jim Maurer says that he wouldn't be where he is today if it weren't for some advice his big brother, Bob, gave him when he was a sophomore in high school. The advice? Get off your duff and do something! It seems that Maurer had spent freshman year in high school just going to school, getting pretty good grades, and hanging out. His older and wiser brother knew that he was missing out on some of the best parts of high school, so he hooked Maurer up with the school's athletic director and got him involved with the sports program.

As it turns out, Maurer was good at math, so the athletic director put him to work keeping team statistics at football games. Later, he was asked to be the assistant trainer so that someone would be ready to take over for the senior who was the team manager. His school sent him to a Cramer workshop at Southern Methodist University (SMU) where he spent two weeks learning the basics: first aid, taping ankles, etc. This training prepared him to finish out high school as the football team manager.

IT'S NOT ALWAYS THIS EASY

When it came time to decide where to go to college, he chose SMU with hopes of becoming an athletic trainer. It helped that his stepsister, a nurse, was already a trainer there. He is grateful to have had the chance to learn under one of the best in the business, Cash Birdwell, who retired from SMU after 33 years.

He started the required athletic trainer internship as an assistant trainer for both the football and swim teams. During his junior year, he got the lucky break that set the course for his professional career. He was chosen for a student internship with the Dallas Cowboys at their training camp. His senior year, he had the chance to intern with the Kansas City Chiefs. As if that weren't enough, after he'd graduated from college and was busy earning his teaching credentials, he was chosen to participate in the Cowboys' graduate assistant program for two years in a row. By this time, Maurer's foot was planted firmly in the door, and it was an easy decision for the Cowboys to name him an official assistant trainer when the position became available.

Needless to say, Maurer has been with the Cowboys ever since. He says he was one of the lucky ones. Most people don't land a job with the pros right out of college. In fact, his all-time goal as an aspiring athletic trainer in college had been to land a spot with one of the top college teams.

ALL IN A DAY'S WORK

Maurer does his best to keep the Cowboys healthy and injury-free. When the inevitable injuries come, his job is to get those million-dollar men back into tip-top shape and out on the playing field as quickly and as safely as possible. He's standing by at all the games and practices to provide emergency medical attention, and quite often he's nearby when one of the players has to have surgery. Since there are usually at least 6 to 12 players in need of surgical repair after each season, his presence at their operations can become a big part of the off-season job. He serves as a liaison between the player and medical professionals, explains the ramifications of the injury to each player, and helps plan a rehabilitation program in conjunction with the team's other athletic trainers that gets players back in the game with all body parts in good working order.

HOME FOR THE HOLIDAYS

The job requires long hours and a demanding schedule. He says that he recently spent Christmas with his family for the first time in seven years. During football season, his work schedule is at least 12 hours a day, 7 days a week. He goes on the road with the team for games and attends the six-week training camp. You've got to love the work to keep up the pace.

THE HEALING TOUCH

Maurer says that what makes his work so worthwhile is being part of the success stories. Two of his favorites involve Michael Irvin and Erik Williams. He counts it a real thrill to have seen Irvin come back to be voted MVP at a Pro Bowl after recovering from a career-threatening knee injury. As for Williams, not only was it a miracle that he even survived the car crash that shattered his leg, but he also came back to play in a Pro Bowl. Success stories like this are what his job is all about.

ON THE INJURED LIST

Maurer says that it can be tough for a big, strong athlete to get used to the idea of being hurt. He jokes that the bigger they are, the harder they fall. Part of his job is to encourage injured players and motivate them to work hard throughout the often painful rehabilitation process. He's made it a point to extend the same level of care and concern to every player who gets hurt, whether it's Troy Aikman or a third-string running back.

SOME WINNING WORDS

No matter what career path a person chooses, Maurer says that the ultimate goal should be to wake up each morning and want to go to work. When work becomes something a person dreads, Maurer says it's time to find another job. Sounds like winning advice from a man who's gone with the Cowboys to the Super Bowl three times!

Coach

SKILL SET

✔ ADVENTURE

✔ TALKING

✔ SPORTS

WHAT IS A COACH?

Coaches are paid to win games. However, the actual coaching of games, the part that spectators see at sports events, is just a small part of a coach's overall job. Coaches have quite a few behind-the-scenes responsibilities. First, there is the job of picking the right mix of players with the hopes of turning the skills of many individuals into a winning team. This stage involves recruiting, observing, evaluating, and making tough decisions about who stays on the team and who gets cut. Once the team is created, they must get the players ready to play.

Coaches work with the players both on the field and off, helping them reach their personal best physically, mentally, and even academically in the case of high school and college coaches. As teachers, they give instruction in the rules and regulations of the game. As trainers, they equip the athlete with skills necessary to compete in the game. As protectors, they do all they can to keep the players physically fit and free from injury. As motivators, they keep the team charged up and make sure that negative attitudes are kept at bay.

In addition to coaching teams in sports such as football, baseball, and basketball, some coaches specialize in individual sports such as tennis, golf, swimming, diving, figure skating, and gymnastics. Others may work as a private coach to just one athlete in preparation for a major sporting event, such as the Olympics or a world championship.

Perhaps even more than with other professions, athletic coaches must pay their dues. Nobody (repeat nobody) graduates from college and lands a first job as head coach of a professional sports team. Instead, one starts out on a high school or college level, and even there it's quite often as an assistant. Many coaches who work with professional teams were once professional athletes themselves.

At every level, the hours can be long and unpredictable, especially during the playing season. Overall, coaching can be an intense profession, since working with players and officials can be stressful.

With all that said, if you're still interested in becoming a coach, plan on going to college to earn a degree in a field such as physical education. You'll also want to make the most of every opportunity to play sports. If you can manage to land a spot on a college team, so much the better. If not, get involved in the sports program in any and every way that you can.

Coaching can be an exciting and satisfying career choice for sports fanatics who want to help other people succeed. It is important to have the inner strength to handle the team's victories as well as its losses.

☞ TRY IT OUT

WEEKEND SPORTS MARATHON
Finish your chores, do your homework, and negotiate with the rest of the family to keep the television tuned to sports programs for the day. See how many different teams and how many different sports you can squeeze into a sports marathon. Use the remote control to bounce around to various events. Keep a list of each team and the outcome of each game. Also make a note of the name of each team's head coach and any details you notice about his or her coaching style.

KNOW THE RULES!
If you're going to coach at any level, you've got to know the rules. Ask your school coach or community sports association for copies of the official rule book for your favorite sport. Or go online to find lists of rules for virtually every sport from A to Z at http://www.everyrule.com/sports_az_list. html. Use the information you discover to create a poster that describes the 10 most important rules for your favorite sport.

✔ CHECK IT OUT

🖱 ON THE WEB
ONLINE COACHING
There is a wide variety of Internet resources that you can tap into to find out more about the coaching profession. One way to do this is to run a search using a Web browser. Simply type the word that describes what you are looking for, such as coaching or basketball coaches or Detroit Tigers, and see what you come up with. Here are a few specific sites to visit as well.

☼ Gatorade Sports Science Institute at http://www
.gssiweb.com offers information about topics such
as sports nutrition, coaching and motivation techniques, and injury prevention.
☼ National Alliance for Youth Sports at http://nays
.org is full of tips for coaches working with athletes
between the ages of 6 and 16.
☼ Sit in the coaches corner at http://www.thecoaching
corner.com.
☼ Plenty of youth sports coaching tips can be found
at http://www.y-coach.com and http://www.youth-
sports.com.

MEET THE COACH

According to the ESPN Sports Century Web site (http://espn
.go.com/sportscentury), the following 10 coaches were the
greatest coaches of the 20th century: Vince Lombardi,
John Wooden, Red Auerbach, Dean Smith, Bear Bryant, John
McGraw, George Halas, Don Shula, Paul Brown, and Knute
Rockne.

Get acquainted with some of these extraordinary coaches
by using your favorite Internet search engine such as http://
www.google.com or http://www.yahoo.com to search for
information about each coach. Make a chart and list the
name of each coach, the team(s) he coached, and a famous
quote or bit of advice he was known to offer his players.

📚 AT THE LIBRARY

ARMCHAIR COACHING

Read all about coaching and coaches in books such as:

_____

Coaches and Fitness Professionals. New York: Ferguson, 2004.
Jones, Janice. *Coach Carter.* Los Angeles: Amistad, 2004.
Minden, Cecilia. *Coaches.* Minneapolis: Child's World, 2006.
Nelson, Robin. *Coaches.* Minneapolis: Lerner, 2005.

_____

Also, keep in mind that coaches need to know their games inside and out. Get into your favorite sports with the information found in these *Getting Into Sports* titles:

———————————

Thomas, Ron, and Joe Herran. *Getting Into Baseball*. New York: Chelsea House, 2005.
———. *Getting Into Basketball*. New York: Chelsea House, 2005.
———. *Getting Into Golf*. New York: Chelsea House, 2005.
———. *Getting Into Hockey*. New York: Chelsea House, 2005.
———. *Getting Into Soccer*. New York: Chelsea House, 2005.
———. *Getting Into Tennis*. New York: Chelsea House, 2005.

———————————

🗣 WITH THE EXPERTS

American Football Coaches Association
100 Legends Lane
Waco, TX 76706-1243
http://www.afca.com

National Association for Sport and Physical Education
1900 Association Drive
Reston, VA 20191-1502
http://www.aahperd.org/NASPE

National Association of Basketball Coaches
1111 Main Street, Suite 1000
Kansas City, MO 64105-2136
http://nabc.cstv.org

National High School Athletic Coaches Association
Norwich Free Academy
305 Broadway
Norwich, CT 06360-3547
http://www.hscoaches.org

National High School Baseball Coaches Association
PO Box 12843
Tempe, AZ 85284-0048
http://www.baseballcoaches.org

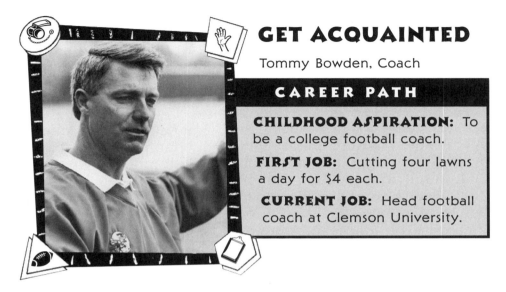

GET ACQUAINTED

Tommy Bowden, Coach

CAREER PATH

CHILDHOOD ASPIRATION: To be a college football coach.

FIRST JOB: Cutting four lawns a day for $4 each.

CURRENT JOB: Head football coach at Clemson University.

IT'S ALL IN THE FAMILY

Tommy Bowden is part of college football history. He is a member of the only family ever to have three college team coaches working at the same time. While Tommy coaches at Clemson, his father, the legendary Bobby Bowden, is head coach at Florida State. Brother Jeff works with his dad as offensive coordinator at Florida State. His other brother Terry, once a college coach too, is now a television commentator for ABC college football. He says it sure comes in handy to have all that expertise in the family when he needs some good football advice.

A GAME PLAN

Bowden says that he knew from the time he was very young that he wanted to be a college-level football coach. In fact, an autobiography that he wrote in the seventh grade lists coaching as his future occupation. Growing up around sports and having a successful coaching role model as a dad helped encourage the decision. But, he's always felt that coaching was exactly the work that he was meant to do.

This certainty provided the motivation he needed to prepare himself for the job—even though it required doing some things that he didn't really want to do. Bowden knew that if he was to reach his coaching goal, he would have to earn a college degree. So even though he really didn't like the idea of more school, he poured himself into his work and did what needed to be done. School was frustrating for Bowden because he didn't see what good classes in math and science and history would do him on the football field. Now he knows that one of the most important things that he learned in all those classes was the self-discipline to do something whether he wanted to do it or not.

Bowden says that since then he's had plenty of opportunities to put that self-discipline to work on the football field. Even in a job you love, there will be parts of it that aren't always fun. Football practice can be one of those things. Sometimes it's more work than play, but it's the only way to get ready for the game. He makes it a point to help his players learn this valuable life lesson too.

A LITTLE HELP FROM ABOVE

Bowden says that it can be a little scary having your future riding on how well a bunch of 18- and 19-year-olds play football. Any coach is considered only as good as his last season. If it was a winning season, the coach is considered great. If it was a losing season, the coach is generally out of a job. And if losing itself weren't bad enough, when you coach at the college level, every mistake you make is fair game for newspaper headlines and the television evening news.

Riding the peaks and valleys of coaching can get tough. Bowden says that his strong religious faith provides the stability and strength that his job sometimes lacks.

CONSISTENT COACH

Consistent is a word that's often used to describe Bowden. Bowden has had the opportunity to coach at several other universities, including Tulane, Auburn, Alabama, and Duke. Winning is something that consistently occurs for his team. Under his leadership at Tulane, the football team enjoyed its first winning season in 17 years, finishing 11-0 in 1998. In

2004, he led the Clemson Tigers from a 1-4 start to a winning season that included playing in a college bowl game. That accomplishment marked the first time that a Clemson team had come back from so far behind to win since 1963. Bowden has also been named best college football coach twice, in 1999 and 2003 by the Atlantic Coast Conference (ACC).

Pushing his players to graduate is another thing Bowden consistently achieves. Since he started coaching at Clemson, 80 percent of his seniors have graduated. In addition, according to the NCAA, Clemson has enjoyed the best record of any other university in the nation for its graduation of African-American players with a full 100 percent earning college degrees.

ALWAYS HAVE A BACKUP PLAN

Although the young men he coaches bring many different kinds of skills to the game, there is one thing that they all have in common. Every single player on his team wants to become a professional football player. Bowden wouldn't pick someone for the team who didn't have that dream.

However, Bowden is keenly aware that only about 3 percent of all college players ever make it to the pros. That's why he encourages his players to have a contingency plan and tells them that a college degree is often the ticket they'll need to make the plan work. He tells them to "shoot for the moon, but if you miss, make sure you catch a star."

Facilities Manager

SHORTCUTS

GO visit a sports arena or stadium and see if you can tell how well the facilities managers are doing their jobs.

READ about your favorite sports arena online. Just use your favorite Internet search engine (http://www.google.com or http://www.yahoo.com) to find it.

TRY following your school's maintenance supervisor around for a while to find out how much is involved in keeping your school building in good working order.

SKILL SET

✔ BUSINESS

✔ SPORTS

✔ TALKING

WHAT IS A FACILITIES MANAGER?

It takes three teams to play many sports. Two teams—the athletes—play on the field. The third team—the facilities managers—works behind the scenes handling the details that make serious athletic competition possible and enjoyable to watch. Long before the games begin, the facilities team is hard at work making sure that every aspect (and there are many) of running a sports facility is handled efficiently.

Facilities managers are the people who take care of all the details—everything from grooming the playing field to ordering enough food to keep the spectators happy. Facilities managers are sometimes hired by professional sport teams to manage sports arenas or stadiums. Other places where facilities managers work include golf courses, resorts, country clubs, colleges and universities, summer camps and retreats, and government-owned recreational properties.

The success of any sporting event—big or small, professional or amateur—is in the successful management of all these details. As with any business, there are several very specific areas that need the attention of skilled managers. One area is administration, where many of the day-to-day details of doing business are handled. Administrators are responsible for things such as personnel, purchasing supplies, and keeping tabs on other departments.

Other areas that need good managers include field maintenance, which is in charge of keeping the playing area in excellent condition; food service, which oversees the facility's concession stands and restaurants; and finance, where money matters such as payroll and budgets are handled. The operations department handles all the nitty-gritty details of keeping the building itself in good shape. Operations managers are basically responsible for keeping the facility clean and safe by monitoring electrical and plumbing services, security, and parking. Marketing, public relations, and sales managers are also part of the facility team. Another team member is the technical director whose main responsibility is managing all the audiovisual equipment that is needed for keeping score, broadcasting the game, and adding other creative touches that keep the audience informed.

As you can see, there is plenty of work to be done. The full-time management staff at a typical large sports complex consists of anywhere from 10 to 25 people. Additional support staff may also work on a full-time basis. During a sport's season, thousands of part-time workers may be added to the staff to handle things such as serving food, parking cars, and selling tickets.

Although a college degree is not necessarily required, a degree in areas such as business administration, marketing, or accounting can provide a useful background and be helpful in reaching management level at a sports facility. Your résumé will stand out from the others if you've also had some experience working in a sports facility either as one of the seasonal hires or in some sort of support position. In many ways, running a sports facility is much like running any other business; however, there are enough differences to make on-the-job experience especially important for facilities managers. As a facilities manager, you may not play the sport itself, but you'll never miss a game!

☞ TRY IT OUT

FOOD FOR FANS

One way to find out fast if you've got what it takes to manage anything is to volunteer to organize a refreshments stand for your school's sporting events. If your school already has a concession booth, this may be as easy as volunteering to help keep supplies stocked and run things during the games.

If this is a brand-new venture, you'll have a little more work to do. First, you'll have to decide on a menu. Simple, prepackaged snacks are probably the best bet: chips, candy, soda, and other kinds of goodies. Shop around to find the best prices on bulk purchases (discount price clubs, such as Sam's or Costco, might be a good place to start). At first, you'll have to guess about the kinds of things people will want and how much they'll buy. After a while, if you keep good records, you should be able to match supply with demand fairly accurately. Of course, you'll need the help of a teacher or parent advisor to keep things running smoothly.

ON THE HOME FRONT

Whether you live in the suburbs, a big city, or a rural farm, your house is the perfect training ground for becoming a facility manager. Think of it as a small sports arena. Divide each of the various "departments" of your home life into categories on a big chart. Departments might include things such as food services (three meals a day), housekeeping (those weekly chores), maintenance (extras such as lawn care, trash removal, and repairs), and special events (appointments, sports activities, and other family happenings). Make a list of all the tasks in each department that are performed on a regular basis. Assign a manager to each department and see if you can come up with a plan for getting things done efficiently and with a minimum of fuss. Make sure teamwork is part of your plan, so include every family member in the plan. After you've had a chance to work out the details, present your plan at a family meeting.

SEE FOR YOURSELF

One of the best ways to find out if facilities management is a good choice for you is to work at a facility. That way you'll get an inside look at what it takes to make it work. Of course, you aren't quite ready to walk in and get hired as a manager yet. Instead, look for opportunities to work as a caddie at a golf course, a server at a stadium hot dog stand, or a ground-skeeper for a recreation center. Do a good job and pay close attention to what your boss and your boss's boss do. That will give you a good idea of the types of things you'd have to do as a facility manager.

If you're too young to get an "official" part-time job, ask your school coach if you can lend a hand as a team manager. You may be assigned various tasks such as taking care of the equipment or keeping score at games. Take advantage of every opportunity to exercise responsibility and self-discipline, since both traits will serve you well in any career you eventually choose.

✔ CHECK IT OUT

🖱 ON THE WEB

MANAGE THESE WEB SITES

Here are a few Internet Web sites that will give you a better idea of both the facilities and the management skills involved in sports facility management.

- ☀ Visit major stadiums around the world via the Stadium Manager's Association Web site at http://www.stadiummanagers.org/stadiums.
- ☀ Find out what real facility managers are talking about by thumbing through online editions of *Facility Manager* magazine at https://www.iaam.org/Facility_manager/Pages/Facility_Issues.htm.
- ☀ Connect to links for all kinds of sports facilities at http://www.sportslinkscentral.com/Sports_Facilities/Sports_Facilities.htm.

📚 AT THE LIBRARY

FRONT ROW SEATS

Get up close and personal with some of America's amazing sports facilities in books such as:

Curlee, Lynn. *Ballpark: The Story of America's Baseball Fields.* New York: Atheneum, 2005.

Owens, Thomas. *Sports Palaces: Baseball Parks.* Minneapolis: Millbrook Press, 2001.

———. *Sports Palaces: Basketball Arenas.* Minneapolis: Millbrook Press, 2002.

———. *Sports Palaces: Football Stadiums.* Minneapolis: Millbrook Press, 2001.

Oxlade, Chris. *Building Amazing Structures: Stadiums.* Portsmouth, N.H.: Heinemann, 2000.

WITH THE EXPERTS

Athletic Equipment Managers Association
1560 King George Court
Ann Arbor, MI 48104-6927
http://aema1.com

Club Manager's Association
1753 King Street
Alexandria, VA 22314-2720
http://www.cmaa.org

International Association of Assembly Managers
635 Fritz Drive, Suite 100
Coppell, TX 75109-4442
http://www.iaam.org

GET ACQUAINTED

Kevin Kahn, Facilities Manager

CAREER PATH

CHILDHOOD ASPIRATION: To be anything but an attorney (that's what his dad was and Kahn thought he worked too hard).

FIRST JOB: Gofer for the Oakland A's.

CURRENT JOB: Chief customer officer and vice president of ball park operations for the Colorado Rockies' Coors Field.

BEHIND THE SCENES

Kevin Kahn discovered a whole new dimension to the sports industry when in high school he was hired as a gofer for the

Oakland A's. One of his teachers had told him that the Oakland A's had some jobs available and he jumped at the chance to get one. He soon found that a gofer does just that, go for this and go for that. His job was to do whatever his boss said needed to be done. For Kahn, that meant doing things such as delivering baseball schedules to sporting goods stores, handing out free hats on cap day, and all sorts of other jobs.

It also meant that he got a bird's-eye view of the entire operations division of a major league sports club. There he learned about the business side of sports and found a perfect fit for his own career ambitions. Kahn went to college to earn a degree in business administration with the goal of working in sports administration. In the meantime, he continued to work with the A's and was given more responsibilities. After he graduated (and his boss left for a job with another team), Kahn was promoted to facilities director for the A's.

He later accepted a position with the Colorado Rockies because it gave him a chance to tackle new challenges in the Rockies' state-of-the-art, club-operated facility from its opening season in 1996. Now, well over a decade later, Coors Field is the oldest sports facility in Denver and one of the oldest in the baseball league. One of Kahn's biggest challenges is keeping it looking as good as new and updating its technology with the latest and greatest innovations.

NO SUCH THING AS OFF-SEASON

As vice president of ballpark operations, Kahn heads the department that is responsible for security, parking, janitorial services, grounds and building maintenance, food and medical services, and guest relations. His full-time staff of 6 swells to about 2,500 employees on game days.

As busy as things get during the season, Kahn says it is even busier during the off-season. That is when he handles matters such as preparing the annual budget, recruiting and training game-day employees, publishing guest guides and employee handbooks, and making sure that everything is in tip-top shape. He manages maintenance crews as they paint, makes sure that all the bathroom fixtures and lights are in good repair, and gets everything ready so that the players and fans enjoy a fun day at the ballpark.

Of course, the hours tend to get longer during baseball season. Instead of the typical nine-to-five day at the office, the hours are more like nine in the morning until midnight.

FUN AND GAMES
Kahn admits that the biggest perk of his job is that all his friends think he has a glamorous job. While having an office at a 50,000-seat stadium is pretty unique, he says the work itself is not all that glamorous. Fortunately, he's happy to trade the glamour for the variety: For him, the best part of the job is that every day is different and full of new challenges. It's also fun to meet some of the famous people that come through the gates.

GET A FOOT IN THE DOOR
Kahn recommends that anyone interested in this side of the sports industry should consider applying for a game-day job or an internship at a sports facility. While there, he advises you to keep your eyes open and learn as much as you can about the various behind-the-scenes functions. Find out about the various departments such as promotions, finance, public relations, and operations to get a sense of where you might fit in. Who knows? You might get lucky and find your dream job, just like Kahn did.

Fitness Instructor

SKILL SET

✔ SCIENCE

✔ SPORTS

✔ TALKING

WHAT IS A FITNESS INSTRUCTOR?

The job of a fitness instructor is to teach and motivate others to get in shape and stay fit. It's fun work with a huge demand for well-qualified instructors. Fitness instructors enjoy the side benefit of keeping themselves fit while helping others stay in shape.

Fitness is in. Armed with plenty of research about the benefits that fitness brings to a person's health and productivity, the medical profession offers some of the best advertising that money can't buy and helps keep fitness instructors employed in all kinds of places. The fitness revolution is creating opportunities on several fronts, including health clubs, fitness centers and spas, corporate wellness centers, retirement homes and communities, and community recreation centers. While the programs may serve different types of clients, they all share the goal of making fitness and wellness a natural lifestyle choice.

Fitness instructors are primarily responsible for developing and conducting specific types of fitness classes. Classes may range from aerobics and water exercise to weight training or strengthening and conditioning classes. Fitness enthusiasts have come to expect well-planned and professionally executed classes, so fitness instructors have to know what they are doing and motivate their classes to keep up. They need to understand the relationship of various exercises to specific muscle groups and other "science-oriented" aspects of exercise as it relates to the cardiovascular system. They must enjoy working with all kinds of people and must possess energetic and sincere verbal communication skills.

Personal trainers, a particular kind of fitness expert, are becoming increasingly popular. Movie stars, professional athletes, and business executives were originally among the elite (and wealthier) group that could afford the luxury of having someone develop a highly personalized training plan and help clients implement the plan on a regular basis. Now, personal trainers are more widely available for a broader audience and are creating some interesting career paths for themselves. For instance, some may specialize in helping to rehabilitate injured or physically challenged people, while others may specialize in particular types of clients such as expectant mothers or traveling businesspeople. Personal trainers must complete specific training requirements and reach a higher level of certification than fitness instructors.

Other variations of fitness instruction include becoming a physical education teacher or a physical therapist. Physical education teachers work with students from the early elementary years all the way through college. A college degree and teaching certification are required.

Physical therapists work with patients who have limited use of their bodies due to injury, disease, or physical disabilities. Physical therapists must earn at least a bachelor's degree in physical therapy from an accredited college. Depending on a person's career goals, going on to earn a master's degree in rehabilitation therapy can be useful as well. Physical therapists work in hospitals and clinics, and some experienced, well-trained therapists may operate their own private practice offices.

☞ TRY IT OUT

HEALTHY HABITS

Think of five simple things you can do to shape up or take better care of yourself. For instance, what about adding some exercise to your daily routine? It doesn't have to be a huge workout. Maybe you can take your family dog (if you have one) for a walk each day or ride your bike to school instead of catching a ride (if it's safe and okay with your parents). Maybe you could replace your usual junk food after-school snack with a piece of fruit or some veggie sticks. Ask your parents or teachers for ideas if you get stuck.

Then make a chart listing each of your five ideas with space to keep track of your progress for seven days. What are you waiting for? Get started now in learning some new healthy habits.

CREATE A HOME GYM

Everything you need to enjoy a personal version of a luxury gym can be found at the local library. There you'll find books about general fitness and ideas for new exercise routines, exercise videos, and information about nutrition. Do some research and come up with a personal training plan guaranteed to help you get in shape.

You can also gain access to some of the best fitness instruction available anywhere via your television set. Check the local TV listings for various exercise and fitness programs. Try

a variety until you find some favorites. Take note of what you like and don't like about each approach and be sure to integrate the good stuff into your own personal style.

✔ CHECK IT OUT

🖱 ON THE WEB

LIFESTYLES OF THE FIT AND HEALTHY

Effective fitness trainers have to stay current on the latest trends and findings. The Internet provides access to some of the most up-to-date information available anywhere. Visit the following sites and start flexing those thinking muscles.

- ☀ Discover five strategies for health and fitness at http://www.kidshealthandfitness.org.au.
- ☀ Do the math on how to burn calories at http://primusweb.com/fitnesspartner/jumpsite/calculat.htm.
- ☀ Take the president's fitness challenge at http://www.presidentschallenge.org/home_kids.aspx.
- ☀ Find ways to get active at http://www.getactivestayactive.com.
- ☀ Take a peek into your potential future at http://www.nmfn.com/tn/learnctr--lifeevents--longevity.

THE OTHER SIDE OF THE COIN

Exercise is just half of a well-balanced fitness program. Nutrition is the other half. The Internet is a great source of informative, interactive, and even fun nutritional resources. Here are a few sites that provide food for thought.

- ☀ Ho, ho, ho, eat right with the Green Giant at http://www.greengiant.com/eating/betterintro.asp.
- ☀ Explore the science of fitness and nutrition at the Gatorade Sports Science Institute Web site at http://www.gssiweb.com.
- ☀ Visit Kellogg's cyber nutrition camp at http://www.nutritioncamp.com.

☀ Climb aboard Dole's Fitness Express at http://www
.dole5aday.com.

☀ Find all kinds of links from the USDA Kids Web site
at http://www.usda.gov/news/usdakids.

📚 AT THE LIBRARY

FUEL FOR THOUGHT

Find ideas and inspiration for getting fit and eating right in
books such as:

_____

Abramovitz, Melissa. *Obesity*. Farmington Hills, Mich.: Lucent
Books, 2004.

Buller, Laura. *Eyewitness: Food*. New York: DK Publishing,
2005.

Goodger, Beverley. *Exercise*. Mankato, Minn.: Smart Apple
Media, 2005.

Hauser, Jill Frankel. *Kid's Guide to Being the Best You Can Be*.
Nashville, Tenn.: Williamson, 2006.

Kedge, Joanna and Joanna Watson. *Fitness*. Chicago: Raintree,
2005.

Mason, Paul. *Training for the Top: Nutrition and Fitness*. Chicago: Raintree, 2005.

Sohn, Emily. *Food and Nutrition*. New York: Chelsea House,
2006.

_____

🗣 WITH THE EXPERTS

Aerobics and Fitness Association of America
15250 Ventura Boulevard, Suite 200
Sherman Oaks, CA 91403
http://www.afaa.com

American Alliance for Physical Education, Health,
Recreation and Dance
1900 Association Drive
Reston, VA 20191-1598
http://www.aahperd.org

American Physical Therapy Association
1111 North Fairfax Street
Alexandria, VA 22314-1488
http://www.apta.org

International Fitness Professionals Association
14509 University Point Place
Tampa, FL 33613-5424
http://www.ifpa-fitness.com

National Dance Exercise Instructor's Training Association
5955 Golden Valley Road, Suite 240
Minneapolis, MN 55422-4472
http://www.ndeita.com

GET ACQUAINTED

Julie Cook, Fitness Instructor

CAREER PATH

CHILDHOOD ASPIRATION: To be a teacher.

FIRST JOB: Worked at the counter at a fish and chips fast-food restaurant.

CURRENT JOB: Movement specialist and owner of Pilates Albuquerque.

Photo courtesy of Frank Frost Photography

A LIFE-CHANGING EXPERIENCE

Fitness became a central part of Julie Cook's life after she'd given birth to her second child. Her weight had ballooned to 250 pounds and she found herself so heavy that she couldn't even bend over to tie her shoes. Fortunately, she was blessed with fitness-oriented grandparents. When she called them to cry about her weight-gain, they sent her a check to pay for her enrollment in a local fitness club. A trainer at the club took Cook under her wing and taught her that there was a lot more to losing weight and staying fit than eating salad and drinking water. The trainer recommended a plan including aerobics to burn fat and weight training to shape and trim her body.

The program (and Cook's commitment to stick with it) worked wonders! Her weight dropped to 130 pounds, and when one of the club's aerobics teachers moved on to another job, Cook discovered a new career. That's because the club asked her to start teaching her favorite aerobics class. It sounded easy enough, but Cook soon discovered that taking a class and teaching one were two completely different things.

However, Cook took this new opportunity as seriously as she had her goal to lose weight, so she started learning all she could. Another friend (and fan of Cook's success story) helped her get a job as a fitness instructor at a back rehabilitation clinic. The clinic offered to pay for her certification by the International Dance and Exercise Association and the American Aerobic and Fitness Association. Through this program, she learned about related areas such as exercise physiology, anatomy, safety, motivation, and principles of teaching.

She worked at the rehab clinic for a few years, eventually reaching the point where she needed a college degree to move forward in her career. Her certification training had sparked an interest in the scientific side of exercise and fitness, so she jumped at the chance to enroll in a new sports physiology program at a nearby community college. She got so involved in the program that the college asked her to sit on the board that developed a fitness technology certification program for the college.

THE FITNESS CHOICE

Cook's career in fitness has had several interesting twists and turns. She spent time working with senior citizens in a Fifty and Fit program. Many of this program's clients, faced with doctor's orders literally to do the program or die, had never exercised before and had to overcome their fear of working up a sweat. This experience was particularly enjoyable because the older students wanted to learn what she had to teach and really appreciated her help.

Cook has also worked in fitness clubs and spas, and she conducts private and semiprivate training sessions for a variety of clients. For many of them fitness is a preventive measure where they work out to enhance their quality of life and prevent serious disease such as heart attacks and strokes. For other clients, exercise is a means of recovering from injuries or other physical problems. It is a challenge to find just the right approach for each client's needs, but it's a challenge that Cook enjoys.

Eventually, Cook was working out so much that she started waking up in pain. At the time, she had been working on and off as a guest instructor at the Rancho La Puerta Spa in Tecate, Mexico, and decided to pamper herself as a guest at the spa for a week. She spent the time immersing herself in the spa's Pilates program and says she had a new body by the end of the week. She recalls that her body was transformed, she was free of pain, and she became a real believer in the method.

Since then she has undergone extensive training in both Pilates and two other methods called GYROTONIC™ and GYROKINESIS™. Now she teaches these methods in her own alternative fitness studio, Pilates Albuquerque (http://www.pilatesalbuquerque.com), to help her clients repattern faulty movement patterns and ease them out of chronic and acute pain.

A REAL LIFESAVER

Cook is pleased with recent trends to encourage fitness at all ages. In a nation where it's estimated that 80 percent of people have back pain and heart disease is a number-one (and often preventable) killer, she believes her work can be a real lifesaver. Her own story is proof that shaping up your body is often the first step to shaping up your life.

Official

SKILL SET

✔ ADVENTURE

✔ TALKING

✔ SPORTS

GO watch various professional and amateur sports games and pay attention to how the officials call the game.

READ the online edition of *Referee*, a magazine for sports officials, at http://www.referee.com.

TRY being an unofficial official. Call a game as you see it and notice how often your calls match the real official's calls.

WHAT IS AN OFFICIAL?

Sports officials are among the most important people at any sports field, arena, or rink. Known as an umpire in baseball and a referee in most other sports, a game official makes the calls on penalties, points, and other rules that ultimately help decide who wins or loses the game. The job demands that officials be "quick on their feet" mentally and physically.

Physically, officials have to be where the action is in order to call each play accurately. In some sports, this means that officials do quite a bit of moving from one end of the floor or field to another. Along with being physically fit, officials must be mentally sharp and sound. There's so much to absorb and process in any athletic event. Officials must be able to match the action in the game with the details in the rule book and make accurate decisions. They have to be confident enough in their judgment to stand by tough decisions even if it makes half of the audience angry. Focus, concentration, and split-second decisions are just part of the game for umpires and referees.

There's one more thing that no official should be without and that is a genuine love of sports. The job is intense and only someone who really respects the sports and the players can handle the heat on a long-term basis. The fact that officials are being paid to be somewhere that they want to be is probably one of the best perks of their jobs.

A college degree is not nec-essary to become a sports offi-cial. In fact, amateur officials who work for recreational or community teams may still be in high school. Many of these lower-level teams are almost always in dire need of officials, so there is plenty of opportunity to learn the basics. All it takes is a good understanding of the rules and a minimum investment in a uniform.

In order to officiate high school and higher-level games, an official must be certified. Experience and competence are the two criteria that determine when an official is eligible to officiate at college level games. Those who have hopes of making it to professional sports should plan to attend special training programs or officiating classes (see training programs listed under Check It Out).

Most game officials do this type of work in addition to other jobs that allow them the flexibility to be available for game days and occasional travel to out-of-town games. Be prepared to start at the bottom and work your way to the top of this profession. Don't worry—it can be done. It just takes commitment and hard work to make it happen.

👉 TRY IT OUT

SECOND-GUESSING

Make it a habit to pay attention to the officials whenever you watch professional sports on television. Whenever a call is made, see if you can guess what it is before the announcement. Keep a notebook handy to keep track of your success at second-guessing the officials.

PINT-SIZED OFFICIATING

If you like the sport and know the rules, chances are that there is a children's sports program that needs your help. Volunteer to help officiate games. Start with the younger kids' teams where the pace is slower and you'll have a chance to learn the ropes and work your way up from there. You have to start somewhere!

READY OR NOT

The work of a sports official can get very intense. As the ultimate authority on issues such as penalties and points, it's not unusual for an official to have lots of people yelling at him or her during a game. Before you decide to become a sports official, find out it you can take the heat. For starters ask yourself the following questions:

- ☿ Do I like to compete and push myself past my comfort zone?
- ☿ Can I stay in control under pressure?
- ☿ Am I confident and able to project myself with assurance in front of a crowd?
- ☿ Do I think before I speak?
- ☿ Am I able to resist the urge to act like a tough guy when confronted by jerky behavior?
- ☿ Can I stay focused and avoid being distracted by noisy crowds?
- ☿ Am I willing to keep myself in good physical condition so that I can keep up with the action?

☼ Can I commit complex rules and regulations to memory so that I am able to make split-second decisions?

If yes was the answer to most of these questions, grab a whistle and get out there! If there were several no answers but you still really, really want to give refereeing a shot, think of ways to learn the skills that are a bit iffy for you. For instance, take a speech class to gain confidence speaking in front of crowds, get involved in a peer mediation group at your school to learn how to deal with wacky behavior, and so on. Where there's a will, there's a way.

 CHECK IT OUT

🖱 ON THE WEB

CYBER STUFF

Pick a sport, any sport, and you are bound to find lots of information about it on the Internet. Use a Web browser to introduce yourself to your chosen sport. Some Internet sites of particular interest to sports officials include the following:

☼ Find links to all kinds of kid-friendly sports Web sites at http://yahooligans.yahoo.com/Sports_and_ Recreation.
☼ Keep up with happenings in your favorite sport at http://www.sportskids.com.
☼ Visit the Smithsonian's Breaking Records, Breaking Barriers sports exhibit online at http://www .americanhistory.si.edu/sports.
☼ Visit a site frequented by real umpires at the Umpire Resource Center at http://www.umpire.org.
☼ Get ready to ref your friends in a friendly game of foosball with information found at http://www .foosball.com.

📚 AT THE LIBRARY

READ UP ON THE GAME

A must-read for all game officials is the rulebook for the sport they observe. Get a copy from the team coach or the league association office. Learn the rules frontward, backward, and inside out. While you're at it, expand your horizons a bit and learn about some of these sports in the Sports from Coast to Coast series:

Chio, David. *Wrestling: Rules, Tips, Strategies, and Safety.* New York: Rosen, 2005.

Connolly, Helen. *Field Hockey: Rules, Tips, Strategies, and Safety.* New York: Rosen, 2005.

Egan, Tracie: *Water Polo: Rules, Tips, Strategies, and Safety.* New York: Rosen, 2005.

Giddens, Sandra. *Volleyball: Rules, Tips, Strategies, and Safety.* New York: Rosen, 2005.

Green, Naima. *Surfing: Rules, Tips, Strategies, and Safety.* New York: Rosen, 2005.

Hayhurst, Chris. *Lacrosse: Rules, Tips, Strategies, and Safety.* New York: Rosen, 2005.

🗣 WITH THE EXPERTS

Major League Umpires Association
1735 Market Street
Philadelphia, PA 19103-7501
http://www.majorleagueumpires.com

National Umpires Association
PO Box 5000
Trenton, NJ 08638-0009
http://www.baberuthleague.org/umpires.html

National Association of Sports Officials
2017 Lathrop Avenue
Racine, WI 53405-3758
http://www.naso.org

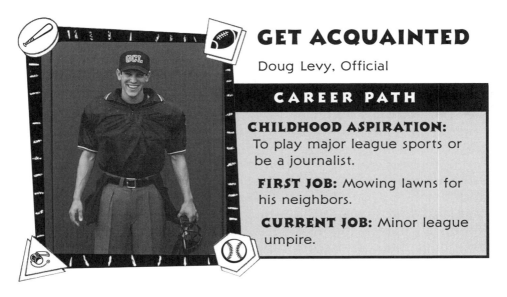

GET ACQUAINTED

Doug Levy, Official

CAREER PATH

CHILDHOOD ASPIRATION:
To play major league sports or
be a journalist.

FIRST JOB: Mowing lawns for
his neighbors.

CURRENT JOB: Minor league
umpire.

GETTING TO FIRST BASE

When Doug Levy was really young, he harbored dreams of
becoming a professional baseball player. A little later he
started thinking about becoming a journalist. Now that he's
grown, he's found a way to blend both interests in some
very creative ways. He's a minor league baseball umpire
who writes about his experiences online at the Association of
Minor League Umpires Web site at http://www.amlu.org.

He started heading down this career path when he was 15
by umpiring games for Little League teams. He completed
a local training course and soon found himself earning $25
a game for doing something he absolutely loved. He eventually progressed to officiating for high school and college
games and found himself wanting more.

His umpiring career was temporarily delayed upon his
graduation from high school when his parents insisted that he
attend college. He successfully completed degrees in both
journalism and finance. But after a short stint as a business
reporter for a local newspaper, he decided that he had to
give professional umpiring a shot.

After a grueling five-week course at the Jim Evans Academy
of Professional Umpiring, Levy made the ruthless cut and

evaluation course and was given a league assignment. Levy says that only 25 to 50 students out of the 250 or so who take the course each year make this cut, so it was a big deal to actually come out with an assignment.

ON THE ROAD AGAIN

For the past few years, Levy has spent seven months a year traveling to minor league baseball games. One year he split his time between the Midwest League and the New York-Penn League and traveled roughly 15,000 miles going back and forth to games scheduled throughout Ohio, Michigan, Indiana, Iowa, Wisconsin, New York, and Pennsylvania. Recently, it was the Florida State League that involved his bouncing back and forth from the coast to the panhandle and other places in between.

Assignments are based on how well the umpire performed the previous year, with the best assignments going to the best umpires. Levy says that he, like most other minor league umpires, aspires to umpire in the major leagues some day. But the only way to land one of those highly coveted plum positions is to work your way up through the ranks. His degree in finance comes in handy when trying to figure out how to get there! Levy says that there are only 68 full-time major league umpires, while there are 225 minor leaguers. The only way to make it to the top is to work your way up from the bottom. Since it typically takes at least seven years of successful minor league umpiring to make it to the top, Levy figures he's about halfway there.

NOT YOUR TYPICAL JOB

Professional umpiring is not like most jobs. Levy says that he usually packs for spring training in mid-March and doesn't stop traveling until mid-October. One year he only made it home for three days during the entire season! The rest of the time was spent driving from game to game, living in hotels, and umpiring games nearly every day of the week. Although he gets only six to eight days off during the entire season, he's quick to point out that he works only three or four hours a day, so in some crazy way it all works out.

Since most baseball games are played in the evenings, Levy has his days free. Depending on where he's assigned, he might spend his days running on a beach, goofing off, or playing golf. He also spends time holed up in his hotel room working on his stock accounts, keeping in touch with friends with e-mail and IM, and writing entries for his umpiring blog. It's not a bad life, he claims, especially since most evenings are spent in a ballpark.

As far as paychecks go, there's good news and bad news for minor league umpires. The good news is that most of their expenses are paid for during the season—hotels, food, and gas are covered by the league. The bad news is that salaries for minor league umpires aren't that great, especially compared to the $90,000 to $400,000 per year that their counterparts in the majors earn.

Levy says that most minor league umpires supplement their pay by taking on an assortment of jobs during the off-season. He says he works for the local newspaper, temps as a substitute teacher, and sells memberships at a gym to earn extra money during the five months he's not umpiring.

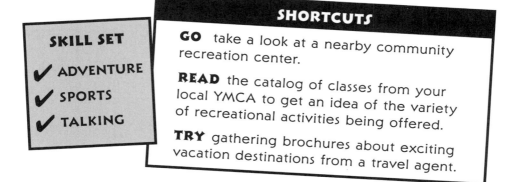

Recreation Director

SHORTCUTS

SKILL SET

✔ ADVENTURE

✔ SPORTS

✔ TALKING

GO take a look at a nearby community recreation center.

READ the catalog of classes from your local YMCA to get an idea of the variety of recreational activities being offered.

TRY gathering brochures about exciting vacation destinations from a travel agent.

WHAT IS A RECREATION DIRECTOR?

It is every recreation director's job to make sure that people have fun. Recreation work falls into two distinct categories. One is community recreation programs, and the other is commercial recreation programs. On the community side, a recreation director may actually work in any number of settings to provide sporting events and leisure time activities on a community level. Community recreation directors may be employed by a city, a county, or even a special district. Some specialize in youth programs and may work with child care programs, while others work primarily with the elderly in retirement communities or nursing homes. Others are employed by the national park service in nonprofit or government-sponsored programs that aim to serve the public.

On the commercial side, recreation directors work for businesses whose main goal is to make money. Places where you are likely to find recreational managers would include resorts, hotels, campgrounds, amusement parks, travel agencies, and cruise ships. Obviously, the duties at these various types of enterprises would vary greatly, but the general idea is to provide entertaining and memorable leisure time activities for travelers and guests.

Whether community-based or commercial, recreation program directors are responsible for developing, scheduling,

88

and implementing various activities. In programs that cater to a variety of age groups, this can be quite a challenge. Activities may range from swimming classes for children of all ages and ability levels to gourmet cooking classes and square dancing classes for adults. A program director must be well acquainted with the needs of the various groups being served by the program and design a schedule of activities that appeals to each group. Successful program directors possess creativity, high energy levels, and a genuine interest in working closely with others.

Some recreation directors specialize in program administration and are responsible for handling the business side of programs. Their duties might include things like budgeting, marketing, and personnel management. Program administrators should be detail oriented, well organized, and diplomatic. Those with an interest in sports and other leisure time activities will find greater enjoyment in working in this type of environment than those who don't.

Additional recreational jobs include therapeutic recreational specialists who provide therapy treatments to help people recover from or adjust to illness, disability, or new social situations. Activity specialists are the people who implement recreational activities and provide instruction in special areas such as art, drama, music, dance, and sports.

There are a number of ways to work yourself into a career as a recreation director. Depending on your goals, you might pursue a two-year associate's degree in parks and recreation or a four-year bachelor's degree in recreation or leisure studies. Of course, it would be wise to get some experience in recreation before making a commitment to college. Opportunities abound for part-time program assistants and interns especially during the busy summer months.

There aren't many jobs that pay you to have fun, so this is one to think about if you are a fun-loving, physically active sports fan.

👉 TRY IT OUT

BACKYARD OLYMPICS
Chances are that on a given summer day in your neighborhood there are at least a few children who have nothing to do. Ask your parents if it is all right if you organize a neighborhood version of the Olympics. Plan an assortment of relays and other tests of athletic prowess. Pass out flyers to the neighborhood announcing the time and place. Make sure to prepare a schedule of events for the big day and have a great time directing your first recreational program.

HOW DO YOU SPELL FUN?
A group of senior citizens probably have a completely different idea about how they want to use their leisure time than a group of preschoolers. Make a chart listing the following types of recreational scenarios. Leave lots of space in between and see how many different activities you can think of that might appeal to each group.

 ⚲ 10-year-olds on a week-long cruise with their parents
 ⚲ Older people living in a retirement community

- Business people at a convention
- Preschool children in a child care program while their parents work out at a health club
- A group of Japanese tourists visiting an amusement park
- Teenagers with too much time on their hands after school

FOR A GOOD TIME CALL . . .

Investigate what kinds of recreational services are available in your community. Make a list of all the programs you can think of and look for others in the phone book. Ask your local chamber of commerce to send a welcome packet—it's sure to be full of information about things to do in your community. You might also contact the city department of parks and recreation to see what options they offer. Once you've compiled a master list, look at it carefully to see if anything is missing. You might also want to use your new-found knowledge to enroll in a program to learn a new skill or sport. Keep the list handy when it comes time to go hunting for a summer job.

 CHECK IT OUT

ON THE WEB
ONLINE RECREATION

Go online for some cyber R&R (or rest and relaxation, as the saying goes) at some of these Web sites:

- Check out an amazing variety of camps and recreational programs for kids at http://www.kidscamps.com.
- Find ideas to make your next summer vacation count at http://www.petersons.com/summerop/ssector.html.
- Investigate how the YMCA provides recreational experiences in communities all over the world at http://www.ymca.net.

⚲ Visit America's national parks online at http://www
.nps.gov and find out how to become a junior park
ranger at http://www.nps.gov/learn.

⚲ Link to all kinds of recreation sites from http://www
.kids.gov/k_rec.htm.

📚 AT THE LIBRARY

PICNIC IN A BOOK

Pack a lunch, find a shady spot to sit, and imagine yourself in
some of these amazing national parks:

Peterson, David. *Denali National Park and Preserve.* New
York: Scholastic, 2006.
———. *Grand Canyon National Park.* New York: Scholastic, 2001.
———. *Great Sand Dunes National Park.* New York: Scholastic,
2000.
———. *Petrified Forest National Park.* New York: Scholastic,
2006.
———. *Yellowstone National Park.* New York: Scholastic, 2001.

For the ultimate in summer fun, see what kind of recreation
you can cook up with ideas found in:

Delano, Molly. *Summer Jobs and Opportunities for Teenagers: A Planning Guide.* Cambridge, Mass.: Perseus Publishing,
2003.
Peterson's. *Peterson's Summer Opportunities for Kids &
Teenagers 2006.* Lawrenceville, N.J.: Thompson Peterson,
2006.

🗣 WITH THE EXPERTS

American Alliance for Health, Physical Education,
  Recreation and Dance
1900 Association Drive
Reston, VA 20191-1502
http://www.aahperd.org

American Association for Physical Activity and Recreation
1900 Association Drive
Reston, VA 20191-1502
http://www.aahperd.org/aapar

American Therapeutic Recreation Association
1414 Prince Street, Suite 204
Alexandria, VA 22314-2853
http://www.atra-tr.org

National Association for Sport and Physical Education
1900 Association Drive
Reston, VA 20191-1502
http://www.aahperd.org/NASPE

National Recreation and Park Association
22377 Belmont Ridge Road
Ashburn, VA 20148-4150
http://www.nrpa.org

GET ACQUAINTED

Jackie Fink, Recreation Director

CAREER PATH

CHILDHOOD ASPIRATION:
To be a teacher.

FIRST JOB: Working at a bed and breakfast.

CURRENT POSITION: Adventure Ocean specialist for Royal Caribbean cruise line.

SAILING THE SEVEN SEAS

Jackie Fink has wanted to be a teacher for just about as long as she can remember. She went to college to pursue a teaching degree and was finishing up her final semester student teaching in a classroom when she realized that she didn't want to work in a school—at least not yet. So she started checking out other options. It just so happened that a substitute teacher filling in at the school she was student teaching in had recently returned from a stint working on a cruise ship. It sounded interesting to Fink, so she went online to find out more. What she discovered sounded even more interesting because, as it turned out, many cruise lines offered activity programs for children onboard their ships. It seemed to Fink that getting a job like that might be like having your cake and eating it too. She'd get to work with children and get to teach, but she'd also get to satisfy her quest for adventure and travel. So, she started asking questions, filling out online applications, and waiting for an offer to come in.

When Royal Caribbean offered her a five-month contract (a standard time length for the cruise industry) to give it a try, she jumped at the chance. Her first assignment was working in the Adventure Ocean kid's program on a ship called Majesty of the Seas. Before she could say "bon voyage!" she was sailing away on the first of many trips to exotic Caribbean islands.

ONBOARD ADVENTURES

For a couple years, Fink's job was to provide onboard entertainment, supervision, and yes, even a little education to children and teens traveling with their families. She says that no two work days were alike. Sometimes she worked as many as ten hours a day, sometimes as few as three-hour shifts. Fink claims that she got paid to "play all day." Depending on the age group involved, a day's activity might include a play, a ball game, some interactive science, or even a disco dance.

During her off time, Fink would hang out in the crew areas, attending crew events, parties, and the like. She says that one of the best parts of the job was also the worst: You were always saying hello to new friends but also saying good-bye to old ones. That's just the nature of the cruise business, she explains, where people tend to sign-on for short stints to see the world and have a big adventure.

She especially enjoyed off days when they were in port at exciting islands such as St. Thomas, Grand Cayman, Barbados, and San Juan. There she'd get a chance to be a tourist like every one else or find time to relax at a seaside café or beach.

BEST OF BOTH WORLDS

After three years at sea, Fink accepted a position with an indoor kids' theme park called Wannado City. It was a new company, and she helped set up programs and kick things off. It was there that Fink realized that what she really wanted in a career was the opportunity to work with kids and programming, blending both the educational and entertainment components with the business side of things. After a year with this company, a new opportunity at Royal Caribbean became available that offers this perfect mix.

Now, Fink works mainly out of Royal Caribbean's Miami-based headquarters, where she manages the managers who manage the onboard Adventure Ocean programs (got that?). She handles the program's day-to-day operations and is responsible for things such as training, budgets, staff, and programs. She also helps cultivate some very interesting business initiatives for the company. For instance, Royal Caribbean has partnerships with other companies such as Crayola to do arts and crafts projects, with Fisher-Price to provide programming and cool toys for the youngest travelers (ages six months to three years), and with a New York City drama company to provide a theater program called Camp Broadway. There's even a program sponsored by Lowe's called Build and Grow, where families build their own mini-ship together.

ALL ABOARD!

So what if you, like Fink, want to someday travel the seven seas? Fink has two bits of advice. One, if you want to work on the recreational side of things with kids or, for that matter, adults, you need to get a college degree in education or recreation. Two, Fink advises that you do what she did. Get online and check out your options, talk to other people about their experiences, and start packing for a fascinating future at sea!

Sports Attorney

SHORTCUTS

GO visit your state legislature to see how laws are made.

READ an online sports blog at http://www. sports-law.blogspot.com.

TRY following news coverage of a big legal battle and see how much you can understand.

WHAT IS A SPORTS ATTORNEY?

A sports attorney is a bona fide lawyer who specializes in issues related to sports. On first glance, it might seem as though there wouldn't be much connection between sports and law. But the sports industry is more complicated than it may look on game day.

First, sports is a multibillion-dollar industry, and big money means big legal issues. Sports tend to be played in facilities that are rather expensive to build and take care of. Then, there are the players' contracts as well as liability issues and tax issues. There are many ways to be sued and ample opportunity for all kinds of lawsuits. There are league rules, labor laws, employee regulations, and even the U.S. Constitution to contend with. In fact, sports law covers such a wide variety of legal issues that it's considered one of the most complex forms of law for an attorney to practice.

That's why the successful practice of sports law is reserved for first-class lawyers. It requires such a vast array of skills and knowledge that anyone other than a hard-working, trustworthy, and truly dedicated lawyer would be doomed to failure.

Opportunities for sports lawyers take many forms. While in some law firms sports law is just one of a number of legal specialties, there are a number of law firms that specialize in the practice of sports law, and some also provide player management services. Either type of firm may represent individual players, coaches, teams, or other sports entities. Individual lawyers may provide in-house legal counsel for major sports organizations such as the NFL, the NBA, the NCAA, and major league baseball. In-house counsel means that the lawyer is an employee of the organization, and the organization is the only client that the lawyer represents. Other lawyers may work for or represent equipment manufacturers, colleges, sports stadiums or arenas, or player unions.

Becoming a lawyer requires some very specific and very demanding educational accomplishments. First, you have to earn a bachelor's degree, which generally takes four years of college. It doesn't necessarily matter what you major in although history, political science, English, and other majors with an emphasis on heavy reading and writing are good preparation for law school. No matter what your major, your grades are all-important. Getting accepted by a law school is very competitive, so only those with the best grades and the top credentials make the cut. After graduating from college, approximately three years of law school follow. Summers are often spent gaining on-the-job experience as interns in various types of law offices. The final step to becoming a lawyer is passing a bar exam. The bar exam includes a rigorous two-day written test and, in some states, an oral exam.

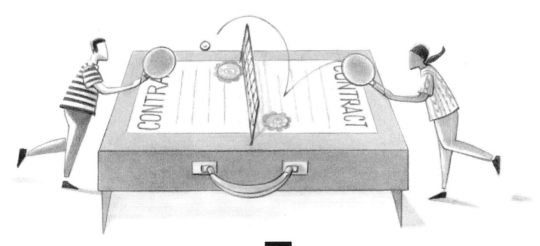

The idea of blending the glamour and excitement of sports with the practice of law is very appealing to quite a few lawyers, making this type of law a bit tougher to break into than other forms of law. It helps to have contacts in the sports industry, a determination to succeed, and finely tuned skills to bring to the profession.

 TRY IT OUT

BOTH SIDES OF THE STORY

Your school debate team is a great place to hone your verbal communication skills, your logical thinking abilities, your ability to think on your feet, and your capacity for completely understanding both sides of an issue while wholeheartedly endorsing a single point of view. All of these are invaluable skills for attorneys of all kinds. Sign up for the debate team now!

Before taking the plunge, flex your debating muscles by making a chart debating the pros and cons of why sports stars are paid so much more money than teachers.

RUN FOR OFFICE

Student council is another way to get a jump start on your future career. There you'll learn something of the democratic process, how rules are made and enforced, and the consequences associated with breaking them. Since laws are just a fancier form of rules, involvement in student government can be a great introduction to the basic "tools" that any lawyer works with.

Think about why you'd be a good candidate and what you would want to do to help make your school a better place. Make a poster to declare your candidacy.

BREAK IT UP

The next time a couple of friends get in a fight, test your potential as a lawyer by negotiating an agreement. You'll want to get both sides of the story and collect all the facts before making any decisions about what to do. See if you can mediate an agreement where both sides come out as winners.

✔ CHECK IT OUT

🖱 ON THE WEB
CYBER LAW

Witness some of the following kid-friendly law Web sites for yourself:

- Throw the book at all kinds of legal information of interest to kids at http://www.lawforkids.org.
- Learn about the Magna Carta, the forerunner of the U.S. Constitution, and its amendments at http://www.enchantedlearning.com/history/uk/magnacarta.
- Acquaint yourself with court procedures at http://www.metrokc.gov/kcsc/kids.
- Visit the U.S. Navy's Law 4 Kids site at http://ogc.navy.mil/ogcwww/LAW-4-KIDS.asp.
- Take a peek inside a courtroom at http://www.usdoj.gov/usao/eousa/kidspage/index.html.

📚 AT THE LIBRARY

LEGAL BRIEFS

Find out more about lawyers and the law in books that include:

Blumenthal, Karen. *Let Me Play: The Story of Title IX, The Law That Changed the Future of Girls in America*. New York: Simon and Schuster, 2005.

Donovan, Sandy. *Making Laws: A Look at How a Bill Becomes a Law*. Minneapolis: Lerner Publishing Group, 2003.

Johnson, Terry. *Legal Rights*. New York: Facts On File, 2005.

Panchyk, Richard. *Our Supreme Court: A History With 14 Activities*. Chicago: Chicago Review Press, 2006.

Parks, Peggy J. *Lawyer*. Farmington Hills, Mich.: KidHaven Press, 2003.

Pasternak, Ceel, and Linda Thornburg. *Cool Careers for Girls in Law*. Manassas Park, Va.: Impact Publications, 2001.

🗣< WITH THE EXPERTS

American Bar Association
321 North Clark Street
Chicago, IL 60610-4714
http://www.abanet.org

American Bar Foundation
750 North Lake Shore Drive
Chicago, IL 60611-4403
http://www.abf-sociolegal.org

National Lawyers Guild
132 Nassau Street, Suite 922
New York, NY 10038-2439
http://www.nlg.org

National Sports Law Institute
1103 West Wisconsin Avenue
Milwaukee, WI 53201-2313
http://law.marquette.edu/cgi–bin/site.pl?2130&pageID=160

Sports Lawyers Association
12100 Sunset Hills Road, Suite 130
Reston, VA 20190-3233
http://www.sportslaw.org

GET ACQUAINTED

Joann Francis, Attorney

CAREER PATH

CHILDHOOD ASPIRATION: To be a teacher.

FIRST JOB: Working as a motel housekeeper the summer after eighth grade.

CURRENT JOB: Attorney-at-law and chair of the employment and labor practice group for Foster Pepper & Shefelman.

A ROUNDABOUT ROUTE

Joann Francis is the first to admit that she never expected to be where she is today. Her career has come together as a result of both random circumstances and careful planning. It all started when she graduated with a degree in communications from the University of Washington. She wanted to be a news reporter and had the notion that she could walk into any of Seattle's television stations and land a great job. Wrong! They all kindly but consistently told her that she'd have to get some experience at a smaller station before they'd even consider hiring her. The idea of relocating to a small town didn't appeal to Francis at all, but the idea of having an unemployed college graduate around the house didn't appeal to her parents either. They gave her two choices: to get a job or to go back to school.

She opted for school and applied to law school as a way of sorting out what she wanted to do. She toyed with the idea of becoming a sports agent but decided that she didn't have the contact with athletes necessary to get started. Upon graduation, she says she was a reluctant lawyer and wasn't really sure that she wanted to practice law. Instead, she got a job as a special assistant to the mayor of Seattle, turned her attention to political concerns and got married along the way. After several years in city government, she and her husband quit their jobs and took off to see the world. Their trek (and their money) lasted about a year.

Back to reality, Francis found a job with Seattle's mass transit system, METRO, and got her first taste of working on projects requiring major public funding. She also gained experience working on issues that involved women- and minority-owned businesses.

SETTING UP SHOP

With expertise in these two very distinct areas of law—public finance and employment and labor issues—Francis started her own law firm. Her work focused on finance and bond counsel for publicly funded projects such as stadiums, roads, bridges, and schools. Later, she and a colleague started a second business, a management consulting company that helped other businesses comply with the regulations imposed by government.

THE SPORTS CONNECTION

Having satisfied the entrepreneurial need to have her own business, when a trusted mentor invited Francis to join the prestigious firm of Foster Pepper & Shefelman, she agreed. This is when sports came into the picture for her. One of the firm's clients was Paul Allen, owner of the Seattle Seahawks. When he called needing some special training for staff at one of his companies, Francis's expertise fit the bill.

As it turns out, all the experience she gained in public finance and employment and labor issues have really fit the bill as her firm has continued representing the Seahawks. They handle matters such as securing public approval for building a sports stadium with tax money, designing and building a stadium, and running the Seahawks' operation.

A WOMAN IN A MAN'S WORLD

Not only is the sports profession predominantly made up of men, but so is the law profession. As a woman, Francis is breaking new ground for her gender. She says that in her personal experience the advantages far outweigh the disadvantages. She's found that it's easier for men to accept the idea that she's a good lawyer than it is for some of them to get used to the idea that she knows something about sports. Sometimes she surprises them by knowing more about the game than they do.

Her experience has taught her that regardless of gender or race, there is simply no substitute for hard work. She says that it's not always easy but that being good at what you do and earning respect for your expertise are factors that can carry anyone wherever he or she wants to go. Francis advises everyone to keep an open mind. Don't limit yourself because you never know where new opportunities might lead.

PERKS OF THE PROFESSION

One of the best parts of representing a professional sports team is that you always have access to some of the best seats in the house for the games! Francis finds it amazing that her career path didn't follow a straight line but led her right to where she wanted to be in the first place—in sports law.

Sportscaster

SKILL SET

✔ SPORTS

✔ TALKING

✔ WRITING

SHORTCUTS

GO interview a friend about his or her favorite sport.

READ *Sports Illustrated* magazine for examples of well-written sports news at http://www.si.com or http://www.si.com/kids.

TRY imitating your favorite sports announcer.

WHAT IS A SPORTSCASTER?

Sportscasters are the voices behind the sports. Part journalist, part entertainer, and part sports fanatic, sportscasters keep the rest of the world informed about all kinds of athletic endeavors by reporting sports news on television or radio broadcasts.

There are several different kinds of sportscasting careers. Some sportscasters work for local or national news stations, where they are generally responsible for covering local and or major sports events, developing feature stories about sports, and anchoring the sports report on daily news shows. Other sportscasters work in radio. Their job might involve providing regular updates on sports news or hosting a sports talk show that discusses various sports issues at length. Opportunities for sportscasters in both radio and television have increased in recent years as national interest in sports has grown by incredible proportions.

Another way to earn a living by talking about sports is as a public address announcer for games on a high school, college, or professional level. This job involves making periodic announcements about the game, keeping the audience informed about who does what, making general announcements, and giving previews of upcoming events. The announcer can play an important role in setting the tone for the game. If the announcer is having fun, chances are pretty good that the audience is too.

At the top of the line of sportscasters are the play-by-play announcers who provide commentary and analysis of the action for televised sports events. Good play-by-play announcers provide so much detail and enthusiastic description that listening to them is almost as good as being at the game yourself. Some of the best-known announcers nationally—people such as John Madden and Bob Costas—are just as famous as some of the athletes they report about.

While all types of sportscasting jobs require excellent written and verbal communication skills, there are some marked differences in the other skills that they require. For instance, a sportscaster reporting on a local news station generally has three or four minutes of airtime to fill with news and commentary. Though it can be a challenge to fit all the news into such a tight time frame, the sportscaster does have the luxury of planning ahead and working from carefully prepared scripts.

In contrast, sports announcers and those providing play-by-play accounts of games may need to fill two to four hours of game time with meaningful dialogue. Their job is to explain each play as it occurs and what it means to the rest of the game. Nothing is more irritating to listeners than hearing some announcer talking about nothing while trying to fill the time. To avoid running out of things to say, sports announcers spend a lot of time studying the game and the teams that they cover so that they have deep reserves of interesting information to share during the course of any telecast. The most successful announcers tend to be the most colorful as well and are always ready with a funny story or amusing anecdote about one of the players.

Another difference between sportscasters who report sports news and those who announce games is the range of sports that they cover. Television and radio news sportscasters tend to report on all kinds of sports and must have a good working knowledge of a wide range of sports. Public address and play-by-play announcers tend to specialize in just one sport and must become virtual experts in that particular sport.

As exciting as it can be to have one of the best seats in the house for important sports events, there is one small detail that makes this type of work especially difficult: the hours. Since sports is part of the entertainment industry and since most people are more likely to be looking to be entertained in the evening, during the weekend, and over the holidays, it makes sense that these times are when most of this work is done. On one hand, it cuts into time with family and friends; on the other hand, many sportscasters ultimately decide that if you've got to work it might as well be at a ballgame.

Obvious skill requirements for any type of sportscaster include an excellent speaking voice, a reasonably attractive appearance for those who appear on camera, and strong writing skills. It is generally considered a plus (if not absolutely required) to have some experience playing a sport on the high school, college, or even professional level.

To become a sportscaster, you'll need a college degree in a field such as journalism or communications. Unless you are very lucky, you won't be replacing any of the big-name sportscasters on ESPN right out of college. Instead, plan on starting your career in a smaller market, where you'll get the chance to gain some experience, get some contacts, and prove yourself.

Also, if you are intrigued by the idea of sports broadcasting but can't see yourself working in front of the camera, consider working behind the camera as a photographer, sports director, producer, or broadcast technician.

☞ TRY IT OUT

IT'S ALL ON TAPE

The next time you go to a sports event, take your tape recorder with you. Call the game into the recorder describing every play as it happens. When you get home, rewind the tape and listen to it. Make note of your strong points and your weaker ones. Repeat this process every time you get the chance. When you reach the point where things are starting to sound pretty good, play your best tape for your school's coach or athletic director and ask for a chance to call one of the games.

PROVE YOURSELF

Good sportscasters make sportscasting look so fun that you can forget there's a lot of hard work involved in the job. Make sure your decision to be (or not to be) a sportscaster is based on the facts. There are two important things that you need to find out about yourself before you head in this direction. The first is whether or not you are a good speaker. Take every speech class you can and get involved in the school debate team. The second is whether or not you are a good writer. Take every creative writing class that you can and get involved on the school newspaper or yearbook staff.

Remember that it takes lots of experience and practice before anyone becomes a good writer or speaker, but if you enjoy the process, continue to show promise, and still think you want a career in sportscasting, then go for it!

TURN ON AND TUNE IN

Writing about sports for newspapers and magazines (the print media) is much different from writing for television and radio (the broadcast media). One is meant to be seen with the eyes and the other is meant to be heard with the ears. See if you can learn to see and hear the differences.

For this activity you'll need access to a computer and a television set. First, tune in to CNN, a national 24-hour news channel and listen to their sports coverage. Listen carefully, and take notes about which games and players they cover.

Next go to CNN's Internet Web site at http://www.cnn. com. Read the written reports about each of the stories covered on television. Identify the main points in each article and check your notes to see which ones were covered on the telecast. Compare the similarities between a televised report and a written one.

✔ CHECK IT OUT

🖱 ON THE WEB

In our sports-crazy society, there is no shortage of coverage about sports. For starters, there are the daily newspapers and television news shows, both local and national. Then there's the Internet, where you can find quick access to the latest news via sites such as http://www.espn.com, http://www.sportsillustrated.com, and http://www.usatoday .com. For a look at women's sports, you can visit http://www .siwomen.com or http://www.gogirlmag.com. All of these sites can provide excellent ways for aspiring sportscasters to learn about the profession. Make it a habit to stay in touch with a variety of sports news sources.

📖 AT THE LIBRARY

LAST WORDS ON SPORTS

Read and write (and even laugh) about sports with ideas found in books such as:

Aamiden, Abraham. *Real Sports Reporting.* Bloomington, Ind.: Indiana University Press, 2003.

Craig, Steven. *Sportswriting: A Beginner's Guide.* Shoreham, Vt.: Discover Writing Press, 2002.

Lupica, Mike. *Best American Sports Writing 2005.* New York: Houghton Mifflin, 2005.

Madden, John. *Heroes of Football.* New York: Dutton, 2006.

Miller, Hartley. *You Don't Say: Over 1,000 Hilarious Sports Quotes and Quips.* Kansas City, Mo.: Andrews McMeel, 2003.

🗣 WITH THE EXPERTS

American Sportscasters Association
225 Broadway, Suite 2030
New York, NY 10007-3001
http://www.americansportscasters
  online.com

National Association of
  Broadcasters
1771 N Street NW
Washington, DC 20036-2800
http://www.nab.org

National Sportscasters and Sportswriters Association
322 East Innes Street
Salisbury, NC 28144-5012
http://www.salisburync.gov/nssa

Sportscaster Camps of America
PO Box 10205
Newport Beach, CA 92568-0205
http://www.sportscastercamp.com/info.htm

GET ACQUAINTED

Van Tate, Sportscaster

CAREER PATH

CHILDHOOD ASPIRATION:
To be a clown so that he could make people laugh.

FIRST JOB: Earning tips by helping older women carry groceries to their cars at a Chicago A&P.

CURRENT JOB: Sports director for KRQE-TV in Albuquerque, New Mexico.

A KNACK FOR NEWS

If Van Tate had been paying closer attention, he might have known a long time ago that broadcasting was what he was meant to do. He says that even as a young child he liked to pretend that he was a news anchor reporting on the latest news. His mother made a tape of one such "broadcast" when he was seven years old (and really surprised him by playing it for him after he'd started his career as a television reporter). He also confesses that as early as eight years old he spent almost as much time watching news programs as he did cartoons. When he was in the eighth grade, he wrote for the school newspaper and really enjoyed it. The clues were there all along; it just took a while to make the connection.

Nevertheless, things just seemed to fall together easily on their own. He went to the University of New Mexico as a business major but found all the business classes boring. He's not really sure why he switched over to journalism; it just seemed like the right thing to do at the time. As it turns out, it was an instinct that forged his future.

OFF TO A GOOD START

After graduating, Tate got a job as a photographer with a television station in Albuquerque. The job required him to videotape stories for news broadcasts. The experience, it turns out, taught him a whole new way of writing and reporting stories because he learned to look at each story from a "big picture" perspective. Instead of writing words to match the pictures, he got the pictures to tell the story, so the words just naturally followed.

He got the chance to start reporting when the Albuquerque station bought a new station in a smaller New Mexico market. He was hired to do some general news reporting for the new station and started doing some sports stories on his own. When someone finally used one for a broadcast, the news director liked what he saw and started using Tate's stories on a regular basis.

After a while Tate put together a résumé tape and sent copies out to other stations. The effort paid off when he was offered a sports job in Savannah, Georgia. After a year working in Georgia, the news director from a station in Austin, Texas, called one morning to offer him a job. He was considering the Texas job when the news director from his old station called later that same day to offer him a spot back in Albuquerque. Since Albuquerque is home and most of his family still lived there, it was pretty easy to decide which offer to take.

BACK ON THE HOME FRONT

One thing that all of Tate's early experience taught him was that he preferred sports reporting over news reporting. He realized this when a colleague at work called some footage he'd gotten about a boy drowning "awesome." Tate's take on the same footage was that it was heartbreaking and awful. He was appalled at the notion of so casually diminishing the human tragedy behind the story and decided to focus on reporting the positive, straightforward news more commonly associated with sports.

At first, Tate worked as a sports reporter, chasing down interesting stories about sports and reporting the results on the evening news. He enjoyed working on feature stories and liked to use his reports to add some "good news" to all the unpleasant mainstream news.

Now several years into a successful career, Tate is a sports director and, as his title suggests, directs other sports reporters in filling three minutes of sports news five days a week. In addition, he is the anchor for sports for the Monday through Friday newscasts.

He says that everyday he spends an hour or so on the phone setting up stories and chasing potential stories. The process, he claims, can be both challenging and rewarding. Some days there are so many stories that they have to save some for another day. Other days, especially during the summer break from school sports, they have to scramble to fill their time in interesting ways each day. Every day the ultimate challenge is to keep viewers interested with a mix of compelling video and reports that are never boring.

IT ISN'T AS EASY AS IT LOOKS

An average sports feature story lasts somewhere between a minute and minute and a half of actual air time. While that doesn't sound like much, it can be quite a challenge getting those ministories ready for a television audience. The process generally starts with lots of phone calls to track down just the right story. Then Tate and the camera crew have to go on location to shoot. Depending on the road time, it generally takes an hour or two to conduct the interview and get the video. Next, Tate has to sit down and write the story. This can take anywhere from a half-hour to a couple of hours depending on the story (although Tate admits that he has learned to be pretty quick). The next step is editing the tape for the segment. Editing involves choosing the best video clips and adding the reporter's story to it, and the process typically takes at least another hour. Essentially, several hours of work are required for every minute of airtime.

Of course, when reporting on actual sporting events, this process gets condensed. Sometimes the crew races back to the station after a game finishes at 9:30 P.M. and has to have the story ready by the 10:20 P.M. sports spot.

LEAVE THE EGO OUT OF IT

Tate offers two bits of advice for aspiring sportscasters. First, make a point of learning every aspect of the business. He says the more you learn, the more opportunity you'll have. If you can shoot tape, write stories, edit, and anchor, you'll always have a job.

Second, remember that humility is an asset, even in the hard-nosed world of journalism. Even if you make it big, always remember what it's like in the trenches and appreciate the hard work of the behind-the-scenes people that makes you look good.

Sports Equipment Manufacturer

SKILL SET

✔ ADVENTURE

✔ BUSINESS

✔ SPORTS

GO window shopping at sporting goods stores to see what kinds of products are available.

READ advertisements for various sporting goods to see how manufacturers describe their products.

TRY making a list of every kind of sports equipment you can think of. Start with football and baseball, and keep on going.

WHAT IS A SPORTS EQUIPMENT MANUFACTURER?

Baseball mitts, hockey pucks, and golf shoes—if you don't have the gear, you don't have the sport. The game can't go on without all the equipment, uniforms, and other paraphernalia that give each sport its own identity. Sports equipment manufacturers make all those products, and they make lots of money in the process. These manufacturers come in all shapes and sizes, ranging from the sports-loving entrepreneur selling T-shirts at a game to the huge corporations that keep the world in running shoes.

If you want a career that keeps you connected with sports but doesn't require that you actually play a sport, the sports business may be just the ticket. To get an idea of the broad range of opportunities in the sports business, go watch any professional sports team play and make it a point to notice everything that is sold there: the drink cups with the team's logo printed on them, the game program, the uniforms the team is wearing, and much more. All those

Sports Equipment Manufacturer

products don't magically appear in the stadium or arena. Someone has to design them, find all the materials necessary to make them, produce them, package them, distribute them to stores, and sell them. Needless to say, that whole process provides plenty of opportunities for interesting careers.

Some of the easiest ways to break into the field are in the sales side of the business. You could manage a sporting goods store or sell a particular manufacturer's products as a manufacturer's representative. Both types of jobs will put you in touch with the products and the companies that make them, and either can be an effective starting point for a career in the sports business.

Another option that might appeal to sports fans who want to "be their own boss" is sports entrepreneurship. When it comes to sports, entrepreneurs run the gamut from the very wealthy businesspeople buying a sports team for franchise to the street vendors selling their products at a game.

Entrepreneurs run businesses that publish sports-related information such as game programs and sports yearbooks, and they also run companies that provide services such as training programs. There is plenty of opportunity for creative sports lovers who have a good sense of how to run a business.

If the idea of working in a sports-related business appeals to you, think about the best way to mix your other strengths and interests with your love of sports. For instance, if you are a real math whiz, think about becoming an accountant and working for a company that makes sports equipment for a professional sports team. If you have strong communication skills, look at working in the marketing or public relations department for a favorite sports company. Professional career choices like these would require the same educational background as for any business: a college degree in accounting for aspiring accountants, a marketing or business degree for marketing specialists, a business degree for future business owners. If you want to work in a sports-related field but don't want to go to college, consider working in the production or packaging side of a manufacturing company, or look into the possibilities on the retail or wholesale side of things. There's something for everyone when you look for creative ways to indulge your passion for sports!

☞ TRY IT OUT

MILLION-DOLLAR IDEA

Sometimes all it takes is a great idea, an entrepreneurial spirit, and lots of hard work to make it big in the business world. In the world of sports, those great ideas have included everything from producing snowboards and specially cushioned athletic shoes to manufacturing protective gear and sports training equipment. Think about a favorite sport and start brainstorming ideas for products that might make the game safer or more fun. Consider a particular sporting event such as a tournament or championship game and come up with ideas for T-shirts and other souvenirs. Put together a mini-catalog of your best product ideas.

COMPETING FOR DOLLARS

There are many companies out there that are making a lot of sports-related products. And, as is true of any type of industry, competition is the name of the game. Usually, each company offers the same product but with a slightly different twist. As a sports player and customer, you have to compare all the different products and find the one that best meets your needs (and budget).

Pick a favorite sport and make a list of the gear you need to play it. Include appropriate sports apparel and the best type of shoes. Then go online and do some cybershopping. Some online sports stores to visit include:

☼ Champs Sports at http://www.champssports.com
☼ Dick's Sporting Goods at http:/www.dickssportinggoods .com
☼ Sports Authority at http://www.sportsauthority.com

Or use your favorite Internet search engine (http://www .google.com or http://www.yahoo.com) to search for "sports superstores." Look for each of the items on your list and compare the prices, the quality, and the claims made by its manufacturer. Try to find at least two different brands for each item on your list. When you are finished, mark which products you think are the best value.

WORDS TO THE WISE

Find out the secrets of entrepreneurial success from some-one who's been there. Chad Foster retired at the ripe old age of 33 after developing and marketing a soft, safe playground surface made from recycled tires. He shares that story as well as his ideas on how young people can find their own brand of success in the book *Teenagers: Preparing for the Real World* (Lithonia, Ga.: Rising Books, 1999).

✔ CHECK IT OUT

🖱 ON THE WEB

CYBER SPORTS GEAR

You'll find information about sporting goods manufacturers and their products on the Internet. Read the labels on some of your favorite sports gear and use a search engine to find out all you can about the companies that make them. In addition, you may want to visit the Web sites of some of the big players in the sports business:

- ☼ http://www.adidas.com
- ☼ http://www.newbalance.com
- ☼ http://www.nike.com
- ☼ http://www.reebok.com

Another Web site you'll want to visit is http://www .cranbarry.com. This interesting site tells the story of how hockey sticks are made. The story includes pictures that illustrate the entire process from beginning to end.

And last but not least, make it happen at these kid-friendly manufacturing Web sites:

- ☼ Dream It, Do It at http://www.dreamit-doit.com/
- ☼ Get Tech at http://www.gettech.org
- ☼ Manufacturing is Cool at http://www.manufacturing iscool.com

📚 AT THE LIBRARY

MADE IN THE U.S.A.

Get the inside scoop on how some of your favorite sports gear is made in books such as:

Englart, Mindi. *Bikes: From Start to Finish.* Farmington Hills, Mich.: Blackbirch, 2002.

Howard, Devon. *Skateboards: From Start to Finish.* Farmington Hills, Mich.: Blackbirch, 2005.

Smith, Ryan. *Golf Balls: From Start to Finish.* Farmington Hills, Mich.: Blackbirch, 2005.

————. *Trading Cards: From Start to Finish.* Farmington Hills, Mich.: Blackbirch, 2005.

Stone, Tanya Lee. *Snowboards: From Start to Finish.* Farmington Hills, Mich.: Blackbirch, 2000.

Woods, Samuel. *Pogo Sticks: From Start to Finish.* Farmington Hills, Mich.: Blackbirch, 2001.

————. *Sneakers: From Start to Finish.* Farmington Hills, Mich.: Blackbirch, 1999.

🗣️ WITH THE EXPERTS

Association for Manufacturing Technology
7901 Westpark Drive
McLean, VA 22102-4206
http://www.amtonline.org

National Association of Manufacturers
1331 Pennsylvania Avenue NW
Washington, DC 20004-1710
http://www.nam.org

National Association of Sporting Goods Wholesalers
PO Box 881525
Port St. Lucie, FL 34988-1525
http://www.nasgw.org

National Sporting Goods Association
1601 Feehanville Drive, Suite 300
Mount Prospect, IL 60056-6044
http://www.nsga.org

Sporting Goods Manufacturers Association
1150 17th Street, NW, Suite 850
Washington, DC 20036-4603
http://sgma.com

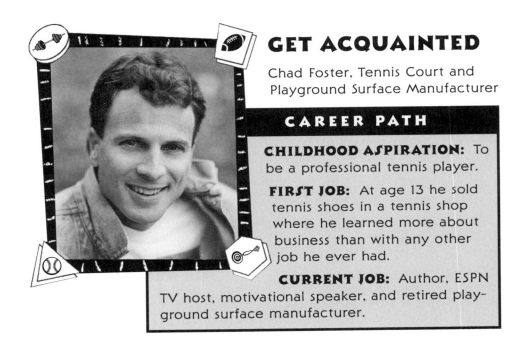

GET ACQUAINTED

Chad Foster, Tennis Court and Playground Surface Manufacturer

CAREER PATH

CHILDHOOD ASPIRATION: To be a professional tennis player.

FIRST JOB: At age 13 he sold tennis shoes in a tennis shop where he learned more about business than with any other job he ever had.

CURRENT JOB: Author, ESPN TV host, motivational speaker, and retired playground surface manufacturer.

WHEN DREAMS DIE

Chad Foster learned how to play tennis when he was 13 years old. Tennis started out as a way to endure a miserable summer camp experience but ended up being a big part of his entire future. It turns out that tennis was Foster's game. He liked it, and he was good at it. As a teenager, he traveled all over the world playing on the junior tennis circuit. After graduating from high school, he went to Florida State University on a tennis scholarship. However, the professional tennis bug was just too strong to resist, and Foster dropped out of college to give his dream a shot. Things didn't quite work out the way that Foster had expected. After a year on the circuit with only $480 in winnings to show for it, Foster knew that he wasn't going to make it as a pro.

At that time, a man he'd met on the tennis circuit hired 19-year-old Foster to work in his tennis court surfacing business. All the people he'd met in his years on the tennis circuit now became potential clients. One of these clients also owned a couple of McDonald's restaurants and told Foster that he needed a safe surface for the playgrounds at his stores.

Foster did some homework and came up with an idea for a soft, safe playground surface made of recycled tire rubber. The resulting product, called SAF DEK, can be seen on thousands of McDonald's playgrounds around the world. It's also been used at the Walt Disney World and Universal Studios amusement parks. Needless to say, Foster found his fortune manufacturing and installing these playground surfaces. By the time he was 33 years old, he was able to retire and ready to pursue other things.

What did Foster learn in all this about chasing dreams? He tells young people that if they have a dream, pursue it, even if it is a long shot. If you don't make it, other doors will open along the way.

A FORMULA FOR SUCCESS

Based on his own experiences, Foster realized that he had learned some things about success that he never learned in school. He now devotes much of his time sharing his story with teenagers all over the United States.

Foster defines success as knowledge plus skills plus people. He says that it's not just what you know but who you know that will determine your success in life. In his book and speeches, he encourages students to meet people, stay in touch with them, and look for ways to help each other out along the way. Since Foster built a multimillion-dollar company with a contact he met at the age of 15, you can bet that Foster knows what he is talking about.

YOU JUST NEVER KNOW

Foster learned the importance of making and nurturing contacts from his dad. When his dad was a kid, he met a guy named Poppy. They stayed in touch by mail for more than 40 years, even though they never saw each other again. Foster's dad went to Louisiana and became a lawyer. Poppy, whose real name was George and whose last name was Bush, went to Washington, D.C., and became president of the United States.

Foster says that you never know. Meeting someone while working at your first part-time job flipping hamburgers could change your life.

GET PREPARED

Foster's book is full of great stories and fun advice, and it's one you'll want to read: *Teenagers: Preparing for the Real World* (Lithonia, Ga.: Rising Books, 1995). Find a copy at the library, buy one from the local bookstore, or order one directly from Foster's company through his Web site at http://www.chadfoster.com.

Sports Event Coordinator

WHAT IS A SPORTS EVENT COORDINATOR?

Major sporting events such as the World Series, college bowl games, and the Final Four basketball championship don't just happen. There are hours, weeks, and sometimes even many months of intense planning and preparation that go into staging such events. Right in the middle of the planning process is a sports event coordinator. The coordinator's job isn't necessarily to do everything that needs to be done but to make sure that it gets done. In fact, a primary duty is to delegate tasks to other people and departments. Then it's a matter of keeping track of who's doing what and making sure that roles are clearly defined, that people know exactly what their responsibilities are, and that everything gets done correctly and on time.

If you've ever tried to get a group of friends together for a Saturday afternoon matinee, you may have experienced in a very small way what it's like to coordinate a sports event. Trying to get several people to the same place at the

same time can require some fancy footwork, plenty of phone calls, and your best efforts to keep everyone happy.

The key to successfully coordinating any type of event, large or small, lies in the details. In a major sports event, the details can be endless: travel, lodging, and hospitality needs for the out-of-town players and staff; special banquets and breakfasts; press conferences and other activities that round out a perfect sports event. Someone has to make sure that there's plenty of parking, adequate security, and a cleanup crew in place after the game. Event planners use tools such as time lines, schedules, and checklists to keep themselves organized. Computer technology has made it much easier to manage all the details.

One of the most important parts of an event coordinator's work is solving problems before they get a chance to happen. Event coordinators do this by thinking through worst-case scenarios, making plans to avoid problems and, if necessary, figuring out what to do in case things do happen. This type of problem-solving action is called troubleshooting.

Most event coordinators would probably compare their jobs to being ringmasters in a three-ring circus. There's activity going on all around them, and their job is to stay focused and in control of all that's happening.

Sports event coordinators may work for a specific team, a sports facility, a government agency, or they may work for a company that specializes in event planning. As you might expect, each type of sporting event has its own unique peculiarities to contend with. For instance, someone who is organizing a major marathon has to accommodate the safety of thousands of participants over several miles of designated course. And someone who is organizing a soccer tournament has to coordinate the schedules of several teams on several fields. And don't forget the trophies!

There isn't necessarily a direct route for becoming a sports event coordinator. Some find that a college degree in an area such as sports administration, business administration, public relations, or marketing proves useful. Others find that they can get a start with an entry-level position, learn the ropes, prove their abilities, and move up to positions of greater responsibility. Volunteering is probably the one experience common to most event coordinators. Getting involved in local sports events and tournaments can provide the on-the-job training that is essential to managing a major event.

There's one more thing to keep in mind as you consider this type of career: Sports isn't the only place to put event planning skills to good use. Event planners also specialize in conventions, trade shows, business meetings, weddings, fund-raisers, reunions, and parties. If lots of variety and having a good time are high on your list of job priorities, this is a career to consider.

☞ TRY IT OUT

PARTY TIME!

The next time the Super Bowl or World Series rolls around, talk to your parents about hosting a big bash. To throw a successful party, you'll need to plan the guest list, invite the guests, plan the menu, prepare the food, and so on. Make sure you think about the details such as where everyone will sit, what to do in case of spills, and how much food you'll need. Keep track of all your plans on a master checklist. Take care of the details and on game day you can just relax and have a great time. Remember that part of a special events coordinator's job is to make sure that all laws and regulations are honored. Keep your sports event in line.

WHAT IF . . .
Just for fun, let's say you are in charge of making sure all the sports events at your school go off without a hitch. That means the players of both teams have what they need to play, the fans have all their creature comforts (as in adequate seating and lots of junk-food snacks), and everybody has a safe and enjoyable place to root for their favorite athletes. Make sure you've thought of everything by thinking through what you'd do in some of these worst-case scenarios. Write down your solutions on a separate sheet of paper.

What if . . .

- the visiting team gets locked out of (or in!) the locker room?
- the snack bar runs out of hot dogs or ice?
- all the basketballs have mysteriously sprung leaks?
- a rowdy bunch of fans get out of hand?
- a thunderstorm knocks out all the power, leaving an entire gymnasium full of athletes and fans in the dark?

If you were the boss, what would you do?

WORLD'S LONGEST TO-DO LIST
Imagine that you've been chosen to coordinate the all-star football game this year. It will be held in Honolulu, Hawaii, and you are responsible for making sure that everything goes smoothly. The first thing you need to do is sit down and make a list of everything that needs to happen to assure a successful game. Don't stop until you've thought of at least 25 items that will need your attention.

✔ CHECK IT OUT

🖱 ON THE WEB
WORLD CLASS SPORTS EVENTS

Imagine you are a sports event coordinator for some of the major sports events showcased at Web sites such as:

- 💡 The Olympics at http://www.nbcolympics.com
- 💡 Major League Baseball's World Series at http://mlb .mlb.com (and use the search function there to look for the latest information on the World Series)
- 💡 Professional football's Superbowl at http://www .superbowl.com
- 💡 College football bowl games at http://football.about .com/od/bowlgames
- 💡 Hockey's Stanley Cup challenge at http://www.nhl.com/ cup/index.html and http://www.legendsofhockey.net/ html/silver_vrtro.htm

📚 AT THE LIBRARY
RECREATIONAL READING

You'll be the life of the party, the picnic, and your next neighborhood get-together with ideas found in books such as:

Blakey, Nancy. *Go Outside: Over 130 Activities for Outdoor Adventures.* Berkeley, Calif.: Ten Speed, 2004.

Gordon, Lynn. *Super Duper Activity Book: Over 120 Games, Projects and More.* San Francisco: Chronicle, 2003.

Rhatigan, Joe. *Run, Jump, Hide, Slide, Splash: The 200 Best Games Ever.* New York: Sterling, 2005.

Ripoll, Oriol. *Play With Us: 100 Games From Around the World.* Chicago: Chicago Review, 2005.

Vecchoine, Glen. *Sidewalk Games.* New York. Sterling, 2005.

🗣 WITH THE EXPERTS

International Society of Meeting Planners
1224 North Nokomis, NE
Alexandria, MN 56308-5072
http://www.iami.org/ISMP/home.cfm

Meeting Professionals International
3030 Lyndon B. Johnson Freeway, Suite 1700
Dallas, TX 75234-2759
http://www.mpiweb.org

Public Relations Society of America
33 Maiden Lane, 11th Floor
New York, NY 10038-5150
http://www.prsa.org

GET ACQUAINTED

Dick Ratliff, Sports Event
Coordinator

CAREER PATH

CHILDHOOD ASPIRATION: To go to college; at various times entertained thoughts of becoming a coach, a cartoonist, an architect, a teacher, and a salesman.

FIRST JOB: Making Christmas wreaths, loading them in his wagon, and selling them to neighbors when he was just a young boy.

CURRENT JOB: Active life director and past president of the Tournament of Roses Association.

THINGS WERE DIFFERENT THEN

Dick Ratliff graduated from high school in 1955 and says things were very different back then. For one thing, he says that there wasn't much time to think about what you wanted to do in life. It was pretty clear cut: get a good education, get a good job, raise a family. That's exactly what Ratliff did. He worked his way as a carpenter and coach through four years at the University of California at Los Angeles. He got married as a junior in college and kept on studying and working. After he earned a degree in political science, Ratliff continued working as a union carpenter for a couple of years until presented with what turned out to be the opportunity of a lifetime. That opportunity was to buy a wholesale roofing materials business. Overall, business was good through the years that he raised his family. So good that it's given him the chance to semiretire and indulge his real passion—the Tournament of Roses parade and football game.

A LABOR OF LOVE

Ratliff has been a volunteer for the Tournament of Roses parade and Rose Bowl game for more than 30 years. He started out manning barricades at the parade. Over the years, he has served on many different committees, including the Public Relations Committee; the Coronation, Queen, and Court Committee; and the Float Committee. In several instances, he's taken on the leadership position on the committee by serving as committee chair. At one point he served as the president of the entire operation. Overseeing close to a thousand volunteers (donating a total of 80,000 volunteer hours each year) and handling a multimillion-dollar budget, Ratliff says his job is quite a bit like running a large corporation. The notable difference is that he doesn't receive a paycheck.

Even though Ratliff devoted between 20 to 30 hours every week to the tournament, he doesn't receive a penny in return. Ratliff says that this volunteer work has introduced him to a whole other side of life, and he's been enriched in ways that money can't buy.

As president, Ratliff was responsible for things like planning the budget, making long-range plans, and keeping in touch with the various committees that run specific aspects of the event. He spent quite a bit of time on the phone and often traveled as a goodwill ambassador for the tournament. Socializing with parade corporate sponsors and big-name sports figures is just part of the job.

A FAMILY TRADITION

Ratliff learned the value of volunteering through the example of his very involved parents. His father was active as scoutmaster of his son's Boy Scout troop, in his son's high school and college sports activities, and in professional associations for his industry. His mother volunteered in cub scouts, the PTA, and business leadership. The Ratliff family tradition of volunteering has entered a third generation: one of Ratliff's sons serves as a Tournament of Roses volunteer, and the other coaches YMCA and Little League teams.

A WINNING FORMULA

Ratliff says that he still hasn't found a better way for preparing for life's challenges than by getting a good education. He credits his own liberal arts education with teaching him how to write and reason—two skills that he's put to the test in his business and in his volunteer activities.

Sports Information Director

SKILL SET

✔ SPORTS

✔ TALKING

✔ WRITING

SHORTCUTS

GO to a college-level sports event and collect all the available promotional materials.

READ the sports information contained in the "virtual resource center for sports information" at http://www.sirc.ca. With links to more than 14,000 sites, it may take a while!

TRY finding the Web site for a favorite college on the Internet and look for information about its sports program.

WHAT IS A SPORTS INFORMATION DIRECTOR?

Sports information directors are public relations experts who specialize in sports. Sports information directors typically represent either an entire sports program or a particular sport or team. Places that employ sports information directors include colleges and universities, professional sports teams, sports clubs and resorts, and sports associations.

The basic goal of sports information directors is to attract attention, particularly the media's attention, to their sports programs. To accomplish this, sports information directors write and distribute a variety of newsworthy materials, including team and player biographies, press kits, yearbooks, game programs, and press releases.

Newsworthy events may take the form of game announcements, team statistics, introductions of new players or coaching staff, and other types of factual information. Sports information directors may also try to "get some ink" with interesting feature stories about individual players or teams or by suggesting angles for stories about team trivia, traditions, or other unusual ideas.

Another area of responsibility that generally falls under a sports information director's care is arranging press conferences, press briefings, and interviews. These kinds of face-to-face informational events occur before and/or after games and when other matters of interest to the public arise (such as a player trade or a coach firing). Usually the sports information director also is responsible for coordinating details associated with televising or providing live radio broadcasts of games.

As with any other public relations person, a sports information director must be prepared to handle crisis situations. For instance, if a player gets injured or in some sort of trouble, a sports information director must be ready to provide reliable and objective information. Sometimes things happen so fast that he or she must be ready to respond to a situation immediately, making effective verbal communication skills very important.

Along with all their work building and maintaining good relations with the media, sports information directors must also satisfy another group: sports fans. Sports information directors produce game programs and other materials that keep fans informed and excited about the team. They may also work with the marketing department to prepare promotional materials announcing games and other sports events.

This job involves a lot of responsibility, and it can be quite demanding. This career works best for someone who loves sports and enjoys being in the thick of things. Preparing to be a sports information director should include college-level training in a field such as public relations, communications, journalism, or marketing.

☞ TRY IT OUT

SPREAD THE WORD
Here are number of ways to serve as your school's sports information director:

- ☼ make posters promoting an upcoming sports event
- ☼ write a story about a star player and submit it to the local newspaper
- ☼ put together a special game program for the homecoming game
- ☼ interview the coach for an article in the school newspaper
- ☼ create a collage celebrating your school's sports programs (use photographs, headlines, scores from big wins, etc.)

JUST THE FACTS, PLEASE
Pick a favorite professional athlete. Collect as much information as you can about him or her, including photographs from magazine or newspaper articles. Use this information to write a player biography. Make sure to include important details such as age, hometown, college attended, and key achievements as an athlete. Use a computer to jazz it up and make it look professional.

THE YEAR IN REVIEW
Volunteer to work as (or with) the sports editor for the school yearbook. That experience will help you get a look at all the

sports programs at your school and to find creative ways of presenting them in print.

✔ CHECK IT OUT

🖰 ON THE WEB

STRAIGHT TO THE SOURCE

The National Collegiate Athletic Association (NCAA) is the governing body of most college sports programs. The best college sports teams in the nation are recognized by the NCAA as Division I teams, which makes these schools coveted places for sports information directors to work. See what kind of newsworthy information you can find about your favorite sports team at Web sites such as

- ☿ NCAA Official Home Page at http://www.ncaasports .com
- ☿ NCAA Hall of Champions at http://www.ncaa.org/ hall_of_champions/global/home.htm
- ☿ NCAA School Directory at http://www.ncaasports .com/schools
- ☿ NCAA Student at http://www.ncaastudent.org

THE NUMBER GAME

Have fun testing your skill at all kinds of sports trivia and statistics at Web sites like:

- ☿ NFL's Play Football at http://www.playfootball.com/ games
- ☿ Sports Illustrated for Kids at http://www.sikids.com
- ☿ Time for Kid's Olympics at http://www.timeforkids .com/TFK/olympics

For a whopping list of sports trivia online, go to http://www .primate.wisc.edu/people/hamel/sportstriv.html.

📚 AT THE LIBRARY

WALKING SPORTS ENCYCLOPEDIA

Add to your top-of-the-mind sports trivia and statistics with books such as:

Buckley, James. *1,001 Facts About Hitters.* New York: DK Publishing, 2004.

Fischer, David. *Baseball Top 10.* New York: DK Publishing, 2004.

———. *Basketball Top 10.* New York: DK Publishing, 2004.

Marin, Matt. *1,001 Facts About Pitchers.* New York: DK Publishing, 2004.

Pellowski, Michael. *Little Giant of Football Facts.* New York: Sterling, 2005.

Stewart, Wayne. *Little Giant of Basketball Facts.* New York: Sterling, 2005.

Varilla, Mary. *Visual Sports Encyclopedia.* New York: Scholastic, 2006.

Varilla Jones, Mary, ed. *Sports Illustrated for Kids: Year In Sports 2006.* New York: Scholastic, 2005.

Wukovits, John. *Encyclopedia of World Sports.* New York: Scholastic, 2006.

🗣 WITH THE EXPERTS

College Sports Information Directors of America
202 Tudor Drive
Ithaca, NY 14850-6330
http://www.cosida.com

National Collegiate Athletic Association
700 W. Washington Street
PO Box 6222-2710
Indianapolis, IN 46206
http://www.ncaa.org

Public Relations Society of America
33 Maiden Lane, 11th Floor
New York, NY 10038-5150
http://www.prsa.org

GET ACQUAINTED

Bob Beretta,
Sports Information Director

CAREER PATH

CHILDHOOD ASPIRATION:
To be a baseball player or
sportswriter.

FIRST JOB: Busboy at a
restaurant.

CURRENT JOB: Sports informa-
tion director at the United States
Military Academy in West Point,
New York.

A HEAD START

Bob Beretta got an early start on his career. When he was
just eight or nine years old, he would come home from his
Little League games and write extensive notes about how
the game went. He still has notebooks full of these stories as
well as his personal accounts of World Series games and other
major league action. Of course, at the time, he had no idea
that this was something he could do for a living. It was just
something he did for fun.

GOOD-BYE BASEBALL, HELLO SPORTS INFORMATION

When it came time to go to college, Beretta went with high
hopes of becoming a professional baseball player. As backup,
he pursued a degree in mass communications that gave
him a chance to work on Plan B—becoming a sportswriter.
Unfortunately, an elbow injury that required surgery dashed
his hopes of going pro; however, he had inadvertently discovered a new "ballgame" in the school's sports information
office. The part of the job that really clicked with him was

that instead of reporting about teams as an outsider, he was actually promoting them as an insider. It allowed him to stay closer to the game and really get to know the athletes.

He'd been working on the school newspaper all along with the assumption that he'd look for a job as a sportswriter for a newspaper or magazine. When a friend of his talked him into helping out in the sports information office, Beretta discovered the perfect way to blend his love of sports and writing. He spent his spare time learning all he could about the job and completed a summer internship at the military academy in West Point.

TIMING IS EVERYTHING
West Point is one of the first places he looked for a job after graduating. It was located close to where he grew up (Beretta has fond memories of attending army football and baseball games with his father), and he'd already had a chance to prove himself during his internship. Fortunately, the time was right for them to expand their office, so they hired him as an assistant. When his boss left for another position, Beretta was promoted to sports information director, and he's been there ever since.

WHO'S COUNTING?
Beretta's office acts as the official publicists for all of West Point's 25 intercollegiate sports. That means Beretta himself and his four assistants cover everything from football, baseball, and basketball to rifle, volleyball, lacrosse, and gymnastics. Some sports have a men's and women's team. The National Collegiate Athletic Association (NCAA) rules for several sports such as football and baseball mandate that someone from Beretta's staff actually attend the games wherever they are—in town or across the country.

For other sports, the staff is able to get final scores and a game summary from the coaches. Regardless of how they get the information, the sports information office prepares a media release for each and every game. Every year they send out hundreds of game stories. That's not to mention the multipage game notes that they prepare and release prior to many of the games and the 200-page (or so) football media guide that they prepare each fall.

Beretta says that his job boils down to one thing: good writing. Anyone who wants to follow in his footsteps needs to know how to write—accurately, with great attention to detail, and quickly.

YES, SIR!

The United States Military Academy is a prestigious college that trains young men and women to become army officers. That makes Beretta's job a little different from the typical college. He has learned to be sensitive to military protocol and to honor the military's chain of command. For a firsthand look at West Point's sports program, check out Beretta's office's Web site at http://www.usma.edu/athletics.

Sports Pro

WHAT IS A SPORTS PRO?

A successful sports professional, or pro, has to be good enough at his or her chosen sport to wow seasoned athletes and patient enough to teach first-time players. Those are the key requirements for becoming a sports pro. Sports pros work at resorts or clubs and teach a particular sport such as golf, tennis, swimming, or skiing.

Sports pros can work with individuals or groups, children or adults. They must be able to instruct, evaluate, and advise both beginners and experts on how to improve their game or skills. A training session with a sports pro generally consists of three parts: a demonstration of the required skills, an explanation of the rules, and an overview of basic safety precautions. After that it's practice, practice, and more practice on specific skills.

The ability to get along with others and communicate effectively are skills that are just as important as athletic ability in this people-oriented business. Sports pros have to keep their students motivated to work hard and challenged to push themselves to improve.

Training other trainers is often part of the job for the more experienced sports pro. Other advanced opportunities for sports pros include running the administrative side of a training program or supervising other instructors.

Certain types of sports such as diving, hiking, and cycling lend themselves to other types of ventures for sports pros (and fanatics). Such ventures include organizing tours and special trips for both beginners and more advanced learners.

A sports pro can also be a personal trainer who designs personalized fitness programs for individual people. Taking into consideration a person's fitness level, eating habits, and overall lifestyle, trainers create an individual workout plan and keep their clients motivated to stick with it.

Some of the very best trainers work with some of the very best athletes to train for competitions such as the Olympics. They work one-on-one with individual athletes and implement ongoing and intense training regimens. Working at this level of competition requires full-time commitment, as the trainer is often responsible for the athlete's overall physical conditioning and training, motivation, and even nutrition programs.

 TRY IT OUT

JOIN THE CLUB

The best advice for would-be sports pros is to dedicate yourself to a sport you enjoy most and play best. If your game is golf, play golf. If your sport is tennis, play tennis. If it's skiing, ski. If your school has a team or club for any of these sports—join it. Learn all you can.

Remember, you have to be very good at your sport to be a sports pro. Enter tournaments and contests. Play on your school team. The more you play, the better you get. The better you get, the easier it will be to teach others to play.

ONE STEP AT A TIME

Teaching someone how to master a sport is a lot like teaching someone how to put together a gigantic puzzle. Yes, there is the big picture of a game well played. But a sports pro's focus tends to be on the little pieces that have to come together to make the puzzle or, in this case, the game, come together.

Pick a favorite sport and think about a single skill that someone needs to know in order to play that sport. For basketball, the skill might be dribbling. For tennis, the skill might be holding the racquet properly. Once you've come up with a simple skill, make up a lesson plan that you, the sports pro, could use to teach someone the skill. What would you say? What kind of demonstrations would you provide? What kinds of games or exercises could you ask your "student" to do in order to get some practice? Put your ideas together on an index card or simple chart.

SPORTS WHIZ

Part of a sports pro's job is to keep students entertained. Since the pro and the student share a common interest in the sport, it's important to keep up with what's happening and who's doing what so that there's always plenty to talk about.

There are several ways to build your storehouse of knowledge. Read the newspapers and sports magazines (*Sports Illustrated* is one of the best in comprehensive coverage of major sports). Watch sports broadcasts on the news and frequent cable channels such as ESPN.

Or, if you have access to a computer, tap into the Internet and visit these sites for up-to-the-minute sports news:

☀ http://www.espn.com
☀ http://www.sportsillustrated.com
☀ http://www.foxsports.com

🔦 http://www.msnbc.msn.com
🔦 http://www.cbs.sportsline.com

✔ CHECK IT OUT

🖱 ON THE WEB

SPORTS TIPS FOR KIDS

Have fun, stay safe, and play to win with tips found at Web sites such as:

- 🔦 Dr. P Body's Sports Safety Tips at http://www.drpbody .com/SportsSafety.html
- 🔦 Kid's World Sports Zone at http://www.usa.safekids .org/tier2_rl.cfm?folder_id=720
- 🔦 NCAA Kid's Club at http://www.ncaa.org/bbp/ basketball_marketing/kids_club/index.html
- 🔦 PBS Kids at http://pbskids.org/jakers/games/sportstips
- 🔦 Safe Kids USA at http://www.usa.safekids.org/tier2_ rl.cfm?folder_id=720

📚 AT THE LIBRARY

SPORTS HOW-TOS

Find out more about how to play your favorite sports in books such as:

Crisfield, Deborah. *The Everything Kids Soccer Book: Rules, Techniques and More About Your Favorite Sport.* Boston: Adams Media, 2002.

Eule, Brian. *Basketball for Fun.* Mankato, Minn.: Capstone, 2003.

Gordon, John. *The Kids' Book of Golf.* Tonawanda, N.Y.: Kids Can, 2001.

Gruber, Brian. *Gymnastics for Fun.* Mankato, Minn.: Capstone, 2004.

Rossiter, Sean. *Hockey: How to Play Like the Pros.* Vancouver, B.C.: Douglas & McIntyre, 2004.

Thomas, Keltic. *How Baseball Works.* Toronto, Ont.: Maple Tree, 2004.

———. *How Basketball Works.* Toronto, Ont.: Maple Tree, 2005.

———. *How Hockey Works.* Toronto, Ont.: Maple Tree, 2002.
Will, Sandra. *Hockey for Fun.* Mankato, Minn.: Capstone, 2003.
———. *Lacrosse for Fun.* Mankato, Minn.: Capstone, 2006.
Willett, Andrew. *Swimming for Fun.* Mankato, Minn.: Capstone, 2003.

🗣 WITH THE EXPERTS

American Alliance for Health, Physical Education,
   Recreation and Dance
1900 Association Drive
Reston, VA 20191-1502
http://www.aahperd.org

American Athletic Institute
138 Darrowsville Road
Chestertown, NY 12817-4305
http://www.americanathleticinstitute.org

International Association of Fitness Professionals
14509 University Point Place
Tampa, FL 33613-5424
http://www.ifpa-fitness.com

GET ACQUAINTED

Abby Derman, Sports Pro

CAREER PATH

CHILDHOOD ASPIRATION: To be a businesswoman in one of Chicago's downtown skyscrapers.

FIRST JOB: Teaching golf to minority kids with First Tee.

CURRENT JOB: Assistant teaching professional at the Kiawah Golf Learning Center on Kiawah Island, South Carolina.

A RELUCTANT GOLFER

Abby Derman comes from a golf-playing family. Both of her parents and her two older brothers regularly played golf together the whole time she was growing up. But, since they already had their "foursome" to play, she spent her time on the golf course just hanging out and riding around in the golf carts.

When she was in eighth grade, she picked up a club and took a swing. It wasn't exactly love at first hit, but it got her interested enough to take her dad up on an offer to send her to golf camp. Turns out that she was the only girl in the camp, but she still managed to beat all the boys. But, as she recalls the experience, the best part was that all the people in the pro shop, the teachers, and the other players were so nice.

The experience was so positive that she went out for the high school golf team during her freshman year. For a while she harbored hopes of making the school's softball or volleyball teams instead, but neither one panned out. So when her mother suggested that if she worked on her golf she might get good enough to earn a college scholarship, Derman agreed to spend a week of her summer vacation at a PGA National golf camp in Florida. That week was when Derman says she fell in love with the game. She credits that experience, a full week of playing golf and meeting new friends, as being the best thing her parents did to further her golf career. She was hooked and went on to finish her senior year as one of the top five female high school golfers in the entire state of Illinois. She also earned a golf scholarship to the University of South Carolina.

UNEXPECTED TURN OF EVENTS

In college, Derman decided to blend her hopes of becoming a successful businesswoman with her interest in sports by pursuing a double major in marketing and management with a minor in sports management. She played golf all four years and credits the challenging experience of a demanding academic load and a time-intensive golf schedule with teaching her how to get organized and stay focused.

After college, she returned home to Illinois and worked as a golf instructor for First Tee, a program dedicated to helping young people of all backgrounds develop through golf and character education. All the while Derman was sending out resumes and waiting for a job offer in the sports management business. Before long she was offered an internship with a sports marketing firm. The internship lasted six months, and by the time it was over, she knew that working in sports marketing was something she definitely did *not* want to do.

When her dad asked her what she really wanted to do, she surprised him by saying "golf." She knew from the beginning that she didn't have the mentality to go for a career as a professional golfer. Instead, her experience working with First Tee had sparked an interest in teaching golf.

After a brief stint training with an Atlanta professional who taught golfers how to teach golf, Derman was ready to go for PGA-Class A training, a must for professional golf instructors. The intensive three-year program focuses on learning the people, game, and business sides of golf. Deciding to join some friends in Charleston, South Carolina, Derman was hired by the Wild Dunes Golf Club, which paid for the training and put her to work in their pro shop.

A GOLFER'S PARADISE

Now Derman is an assistant golf professional at a beautiful resort on Kiawah Island, home to five world-class golf courses. She works at the Turtle Point Learning Center, where she devotes most of her time to women and kids—teaching private lessons, running clinics, hosting golf academies, and the like.

For young golfers (or wannabe golfers) who would like to someday have a job like hers, Derman has five suggestions:

1. Play the game.
2. Encourage others to play the game.
3. Stay in school and focus on both your academics and learning the game.

4. Mind your manners and learn the rules of playing golf.
5. Keep it fun and avoid putting too much pressure on yourself.

And, one more thing. She suggests that you check out opportunities available through First Tee (http://www .thefirsttee.org) and Play Golf America (http:/www.play golfamerica.com).

Sportswriter

SHORTCUTS

GO join the school newspaper or yearbook club.

READ some of the well-written sports articles in *USA Today* (click "sports" at http://www.usatoday.com).

TRY getting involved in sports—playing them, watching them, and reading about them.

WHAT IS A SPORTSWRITER?

Sportswriters are journalists who attend sports events and write stories about what happens. They interview players and coaches, keep track of wins and losses, and research background information. Sportswriters may report on stories for print media, such as small or large newspapers, magazines, or online news services. Other sports journalists report on sports events for broadcast media such as television or radio.

As other types of reporters do, sportswriters generally work on two types of stories. Beat writers cover certain teams or certain sports and report day-of-the-game stories. They have to stay on top of breaking news and write pieces that are interesting, informative, and accurate. Larger papers or television stations assign specific "beats" for specific journalists to cover. Obviously, the more experience and talent a reporter has, the more exciting assignments he or she receives.

Columnists write feature stories and opinion pieces about their area of expertise. Instead of covering specific games, they might write about specific players or the sports industry in general. Creativity and a nose for news are key skills of a good columnist.

While deadlines come quickly for all types of sports journalists, there is even more pressure on broadcast reporters who often must provide on-the-spot coverage and analysis of various sporting events. With little time to organize their thoughts and no time to edit out mistakes, these reporters must think fast on their feet and have an in-depth knowledge of the sport and the players that they are reporting about.

Similar to other types of journalists, those who specialize in sports generally have a college degree in an area such as journalism, mass communication, or English. Getting as much on-the-job experience as possible while getting an education helps always to boost the résumé.

Sportswriting is a fast-paced and competitive game. It's just the job for inquisitive sports fans who can sniff out a story and write it so well that readers find it the next best thing to being there themselves.

☞ TRY IT OUT

THE WRITE STUFF

Two ideas here. First, attend a sports event at your school or in your community, notebook in hand. Take notes about the game's highlights and lowlights, hot plays, big errors, etc. After the game, write up a hot-off-the-press sports story about all the action.

Second, tune in to watch one of your favorite sports teams play, once again with notebook in hand. Scribble down stats, interesting quotes, and the same kind of information you recorded at the local game. This time, write up your story and then go online to a sports Web site such as Sports Illustrated (http://www.si.com), ESPN (http://www.espn.com) or CNN Sports (http://www.cnn.sports.com) and compare your story with those posted by professional sports writers online. Did you cover similar facts?

SPORTS DICTIONARY

Okay, sportswriters, sharpen your pencils, grab a stack of blank index cards, and get ready to create your very own sports dictionary. Start with the following list of sports (feel free to add your ideas) and describe the basic gist of what each game is all about:

- Baseball
- Basketball
- Boxing
- Cricket
- Football
- Golf
- Gymnastics
- Hockey
- Lacrosse
- Polo
- Rugby
- Soccer
- Squash
- Tennis
- Volleyball

TALK THE TALK

Have you ever noticed how many unusual ways sportscasters have of saying the same thing? A team doesn't win a game; they "dominate" it. The other team doesn't lose the game; they're "creamed" or "decimated."

Get a notebook and keep a log of the phrases you hear on the news and read in the paper. Keep your collection handy, and use them to spice up your own reports.

✔ CHECK IT OUT

🖱 ON THE WEB

ROUND-THE-CLOCK COVERAGE

Log on the Internet anytime, day or night, for the latest sports news. Here are some sites to visit first for a look at the world of sports:

- 💡 http://www.sportsillustrated.com
- 💡 http://www.espn.com

The following Web sites will take you directly to the national headquarters of some of your favorite sports leagues:

- 💡 http://www.afl.com
- 💡 http://www.nba.com
- 💡 http://www.mlb.com
- 💡 http://www.nfl.com
- 💡 http://www.nhl.com
- 💡 http://www.pga.com

📚 AT THE LIBRARY

SPORTS WRITER FOR HIRE

In addition to writing for magazines and newspapers, some sportswriters write books and some, like author Jim Buckley, are quite prolific. Buckley says that the secret to being a good sports writer is knowing a lot about lots of different sports because the "more you know, the better you can write about it." Buckley has written sports books for kids and adults—everything from early readers to a set of sports encyclopedias. Some are fiction, but most are nonfiction. Following is a partial list of the sports books he's written recently:

Buckley, James, Jr. *Eyewitness: NASCAR*. New York: DK Publishing, 2005.
———. *NBA on the Inside*. New York: Scholastic, 2003.
———. *Perfect: The Inside Story of Baseball's Sixteen Perfect Games*. Chicago: Triumph Books, 2002.

———. *Soccer Superwomen.* Chanhassen, Minn.: Children's World, 2006.

———. *Sports in America: 1900–1919.* New York: Facts On File, 2004.

———. *Strike Out King.* New York: DK Publishing, 2005.

Buckley, James, Jr., and David Fischer. *Greatest Sports Rivalries: 25 of the Most Intense and Historic Battles Ever.* New York: Barnes and Noble, 2005.

🗣️ WITH THE EXPERTS

American Sportcasters Association
225 Broadway, Suite 2030
New York, NY 10007
http://www.americansportscastersonline.com

Dow Jones Newspaper Fund
PO Box 300
Princeton, NJ 08543-0300
http://djnewspaperfund.dowjones.com/fund

National Newspaper Association
PO Box 7540
Columbia, MO 65205-7540
http://www.nna.org

Newspaper Association of America
1921 Gallows Road, Suite 600
Vienna, VA 22182-3900
http://www.naa.org

Newspaper Guild
501 Third Street, NW, 6th Floor
Washington, DC 20001-2760
http://www.newsguild.org

Society of Professional Journalists
3909 North Meridian Street
Indianapolis, IN 46208-4011
http://www.spj.org

GET ACQUAINTED

Debbie Becker, Journalist

CAREER PATH

CHILDHOOD ASPIRATION: To be a forest ranger.

FIRST JOB: Worked as a gofer for the *Washington Post*.

CURRENT JOB: Sports reporter for *USA Today*.

Debbie Becker and friend at the 1998 Winter Olympics in Japan.

THE RIGHT PLACE AT THE RIGHT TIME

Along with a talent for writing and knowledge of a number of sports, Debbie Becker also has a knack for being in the right place at the right time. She landed a job with the *Washington Post* by joking with a friend to put in a good word for her with his editor. He did, and she got a job.

USA Today, Becker's current employer, was just a new, upstart newspaper when she graduated from college. Today the paper is read by some 2 million readers every weekday.

ME AND MY BIG MOUTH!

As a freshman hockey player at the American University in Washington, D.C., Becker was disappointed to find out that the school paper covered only men's sports events. When she went to the office to complain, she found out that the only reason women's sports weren't covered was because there was no one to write the stories. Becker volunteered to start reporting about these neglected events, discovered she liked it, and a career was born.

Sports is still a male-dominated world, and Becker often finds herself the only woman in the press box at many events.

To get where she is today, Becker has had to work extra hard and watch her step, but she wouldn't trade the experience for anything.

OLYMPIC-SIZED BEAT
Becker has reported on five Olympic events including competitions in Nagano, Japan; Calary, Canada; Barcelona, Spain; Atlanta, Georgia; and Salt Lake City, Utah. She specializes in covering gymnastics, figure skating, and cycling events. This beat involves more than just covering the Olympic games. Long before the world gathers to compete, there are trials and national championships to keep track of. Becker particularly likes doing stories on unknown athletes in minor sports and on women athletes because it gives her a chance to recognize people who've worked hard and are often overlooked.

THIS JOB HAS PERKS
Olympics, World Series, Super Bowl—Becker has been there, done that, seen it. As a journalist, Becker gets to see for free events that other people have to pay lots of money for, if they can get tickets at all.

ADVICE TO FUTURE SPORTS JOURNALISTS
Get all the internship experience you can so that you can find out what you like and what you're good at. Becker had originally planned to get into television broadcasting, but an internship experience taught her that she didn't like it at all, so she refocused her attention on newspapers.

MAKE A SPORTY DETOUR!

Becoming a professional sports player is just one way to build a career around sports. You can add a sports element to virtually any job you might choose. For instance, accountants can work for sports teams, doctors can specialize in sports medicine, retailers can sell sports equipment and uniforms, and so on. In addition, there are quite a number of careers where a particular sport or team is central to the job. Play around with some of the following sports career ideas.

A WORLD OF SPORTS CAREERS

JOIN THE TEAM

Here are a few jobs where a particular sport (or a number of sports) is the name of the game. Each offers a unique way to make sports a central focus of your career without actually playing the game yourself.

athletic director

cheerleader

coach

equipment manager

official

referee

scoreboard operator

scout

sports administrator

team manager

umpire

MAKE SPORTS YOUR BUSINESS

In the area of business, again sports are front and center. The catch is that your business savvy and other professional skills have as much or more to do with your success in these careers as does your love of sports.

agent

business manager

equipment designer

event coordinator

health club manager

marketing director

retailer

sports store manager

ticket manager

SPREAD THE WORD

Pick one of these jobs and you won't have to keep quiet about being a sports fanatic. Each requires a special ability to articulate the finer points of the game.

announcer   photographer
broadcaster   sportscaster
journalist

TEACH IT

What better way to share your love of a particular sport than to teach others how to enjoy it. Here are just a few ideas to get you thinking.

aerobics instructor   lifeguard
aquatics specialist   nutritionist
dance instructor   personal trainer
fitness trainer   physical education teacher
gymnastics instructor   sports pro

ADVENTURE IN THE GREAT OUTDOORS

Just in case you are one of those sports fanatics who prefer hanging out in the great outdoors to the gym, here are a couple of ideas to consider.

camp director   forester
ecotourism developer   park ranger
fish and game warden   river guide

DON'T STOP NOW!

GO FOR IT!

It's been a fast-paced trip so far. Take a break, regroup, and look at all the progress you've made.

1st Stop: Discover
You discovered some personal interests and natural abilities that you can start building a career around.

2nd Stop: Explore
You've explored an exciting array of career opportunities in these fields. You're now aware that your career can involve either a specialized area with many educational requirements or that it may involve a practical application of skills with a minimum of training and experience.

At this point, you've found a couple careers that make you wonder, "Is this a good option for me?" Now it's time to put it all together and make an informed, intelligent choice. It's time to get a sense of what it might be like to have a job like the one(s) you're considering. In other words, it's time to move on to step three and do a little experimenting with success.

3rd Stop: Experiment

By the time you finish this section, you'll have reached one of three points in the career planning process.

1. **Green light!** You found it. No need to look any further. This is the career for you. (This may happen to a lucky few. Don't worry if it hasn't happened yet for you. This whole process is about exploring options, experimenting with ideas, and, eventually, making the best choice for you.)

2. **Yellow light!** Close but not quite. You seem to be on the right path, but you haven't nailed things down for sure. (This is where many people your age end up, and it's a good place to be. You've learned what it takes to really check things out. Hang in there. Your time will come.)

3. **Red light!** Whoa! No doubt about it, this career just isn't for you. (Congratulations! Aren't you glad you found out now and not after you'd spent four years in college preparing for this career? Your next stop: Make a U-turn and start this process over with another career.)

Here's a sneak peek at what you'll be doing in the next section.

☤ First, you'll pick a favorite career idea (or two or three).
☤ Second, you'll link up with a whole world of great information about that career on the Internet (it's easier than you think).
☤ Third, you'll snoop around the library to find answers to the top 10 things you've just got to know about your future career.
☤ Fourth, you'll either write a letter or use the Internet to request information from a professional organization associated with this career.
☤ Fifth, you'll chat on the phone to conduct a telephone interview.

After all that you'll (finally!) be ready to put it all together in your very own Career Ideas for Kids career profile (see page 170).

Hang on to your hats and get ready to make tracks!

#1 NARROW DOWN YOUR CHOICES

You've been introduced to quite a few sports-related career ideas. You may also have some ideas of your own to add. Which ones appeal to you the most?

Write your top three choices in the spaces below. (Sorry if this is starting to sound like a broken record, but if this book does not belong to you, write your responses on a separate sheet of paper.)

1. _____

2. _____

3. _____

#2 SURF THE NET

With the Internet, you have a world of information at your fingertips. The Internet has something for everyone, and it's getting easier to access all the time. An increasing number of libraries and schools are offering access to the Internet on their computers, or you may have a computer at home.

A typical career search will land everything from the latest news on developments in the field and course notes from universities to museum exhibits, interactive games, educational activities, and more. You just can't beat the timeliness or the variety of information available on the Web.

One of the easiest ways to track down this information is to use an Internet search engine, such as Yahoo! Simply type the topic you are looking for, and in a matter of seconds you'll have a list of options from around the world. For instance, if you are looking for information about companies that make candy, use the words "candy manufacturer" to start your search. It's fun to browse—you never know what you'll come up with.

Before you link up, keep in mind that many of these sites are geared toward professionals who are already working in a particular field. Some of the sites can get pretty technical. Just use the experience as a chance to nose around the field, hang out with the people who are tops in the field, and think about whether or not you'd like to be involved in a profession like that.

Specific sites to look for are the following:

Professional associations. Find out about what's happening in the field, conferences, journals, and other helpful tidbits.

Schools that specialize in this area. Many include research tools, introductory courses, and all kinds of interesting information.

Government agencies. Quite a few are going high-tech with lots of helpful resources.

Web sites hosted by experts in the field (this seems to be a popular hobby among many professionals). These Web sites are often as entertaining as they are informative.

If you're not sure where to go, just start clicking around. Sites often link to other sites. You may want to jot down notes about favorite sites. Sometimes you can even print information that isn't copyright protected; try the print option and see what happens.

Be prepared: Surfing the Internet can be an addicting habit! There is so much awesome information. It's a fun way to focus on your future.

Write the addresses of the three best Web sites that you find during your search in the space below (or on a separate sheet of paper if this book does not belong to you).

1. _____

2. _____

3. _____

#3 SNOOP AT THE LIBRARY

Take your list of favorite career ideas, a notebook, and a helpful adult with you to the library. When you get there, go to the reference section and ask the librarian to help you find books about careers. Most libraries will have at least one set

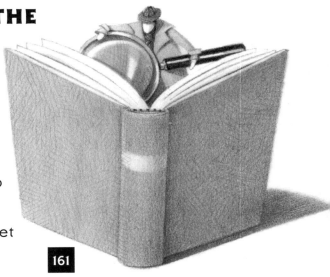

of career encyclopedias. Some of the larger libraries may also have career information on CD-ROM.

Gather all the information you can and use it to answer the following questions in your notebook about each of the careers on your list. Make sure to ask for help if you get stuck.

TOP 10 THINGS YOU NEED TO KNOW ABOUT YOUR CAREER

1. What is the purpose of this job?

   _____

2. What kind of place is this type of work usually done in? For example, would I work mostly in a busy office, outdoors, or in a laboratory?

   _____

3. What kind of time is required to do this job? For instance, is the job usually performed during regular daytime business hours or do people work various shifts around the clock?

   _____

4. What kinds of tools are used to do this job?

   _____

5. In what ways does this job involve working with other people?

   _____

6. What kind of preparation does a person need to qualify for this job?

   _____

7. What kinds of skills and abilities are needed to be successful in this type of work?

_____

8. What's a typical day on the job like?

_____

_____

9. How much money can I expect to earn as a beginner?

_____

10. What kind of classes do I need to take in high school to get ready for this type of work?

_____

#4 GET IN TOUCH WITH THE EXPERTS

One of the best places to find information about a particular career is a professional organization devoted especially to that career. After all, these organizations are full of the best and the brightest professionals working in that particular field. Who could possibly know more about how the work gets done? There are more than 450,000 organizations in the United States, so there is bound to be an association related to just about any career you can possibly imagine.

There are a couple ways you can find these organizations:

1. Look at the "Check It Out—With the Experts" list following a career you found especially interesting in the Take A Trip! section of this book.

2. Go online and use your favorite search engine (such as http://www.google.com or http://yahoo.com) to find professional associations related to a career you are

interested in. You might use the name of the career, plus the words "professional association" to start your search. You're likely to find lots of useful information online, so keep looking until you hit pay dirt.

3. Go to the reference section of your public library and ask the librarian to help you find a specific type of association in a reference book called *Encyclopedia of Associations* (Farmington Hills, Mich.: Thomson Gale) Or, if your library has access to it, the librarian may suggest using an online database called *Associations Unlimited* (Farmington Hills, Mich.: Thomson Gale).

Once you've tracked down a likely source of information, there are two ways to get in touch with a professional organization.

1. Send an e-mail.

Most organizations include a "contact us" button on their Web sites. Sometimes this e-mail is directed to a webmaster or a customer service representative. An e-mail request might look something like this:

Subject: Request for Information
Date: 2/1/2008 3:18:41 PM Eastern Standard Time
From: janedoe@mycomputer.com
To: webmaster@candyloversassociation.org

I am a fifth-grade student, and I am interested in learning more about careers for candy lovers. Would you please send me any information you have about what people do in your industry?

Thank you very much.
Jane Doe

2. Write a letter requesting information.

Your letter should be either typed on a computer or written in your best handwriting. It should include the date, the complete address of the organization you are contacting, a salutation or greeting, a brief

description of your request, and a signature. Make sure to include an address where the organization can reach you with a reply. Something like the following letter would work just fine.

> Dear Sir or Madam:
>
> I am a fifth-grade student, and I would like to learn more about what it is like to work in the candy lover profession. Would you please send me information about careers? My address is 456 Main Street, Anytown, USA 54321.
>
> Thank you very much.
>
> Sincerely,
> Jane Doe

Write the names and addresses of the professional organizations you discover on a separate sheet of paper.

#5 CHAT ON THE PHONE

Talking to a seasoned professional—someone who experiences the job day in and day out—can be a great way to get the inside story on what a career is all about. Fortunately for you, the experts in any career field can be as close as the nearest telephone.

Sure, it can be a bit scary calling up an adult whom you don't know. But two things are in your favor:

1. They can't see you. The worst thing they can do is hang up on you, so just relax and enjoy the conversation.

2. They'll probably be happy to talk to you about their job. In fact, most people will be flattered that you've called. If you happen to contact someone who seems reluctant to talk, thank them for their time and try someone else.

Here are a few pointers to help make your telephone interview a success:

- ☼ Mind your manners and speak clearly.
- ☼ Be respectful of their time and position.
- ☼ Be prepared with good questions and take notes as you talk.

One more common sense reminder: be careful about giving out your address and DO NOT arrange to meet anyone you don't know without your parents' supervision.

TRACKING DOWN CAREER EXPERTS

You might be wondering by now how to find someone to interview. Have no fear! It's easy if you're persistent. All you have to do is ask. Ask the right people and you'll have a great lead in no time.

A few of the people to ask and sources to turn to are:

Your parents. They may know someone (or know someone who knows someone) who has just the kind of job you're looking for.

Your friends and neighbors. You might be surprised to find out how many interesting jobs these people have when you start asking them what they (or their parents) do for a living.

Librarians. Since you've already figured out what kinds of companies employ people in your field of interest, the next step is to ask for information about local employers. Although it's a bit cumbersome to use, a big volume called *Contacts Influential* can provide this kind of information.

Professional associations. Call, e-mail, or write to the professional associations you discovered using the activity on pages 163 to 165 and ask for recommendations.

Chambers of commerce. The local chamber of commerce probably has a directory of employers, their specialties, and their phone numbers. Call the chamber, explain what you are looking for, and give them a chance to help their future workforce.

Newspaper and magazine articles. Find an article about the subject you are interested in. Chances are pretty good that it will mention the name of at least one expert in the field. The article probably won't include the person's phone number (that would be too easy), so you'll have to look for clues. Common clues include the name of the company that they work for, the town that they live in, and if the person is an author, the name of their publisher. Make a few phone calls and track them down (if long distance calls are involved, make sure to get your parents' permission first).

INQUIRING KIDS WANT TO KNOW

Before you make the call, make a list of questions to ask. You'll cover more ground if you focus on using the five W's (and the H) that you've probably heard about in your creative writing classes: Who? What? Where? When? How? and Why? For example:

1. Whom do you work for?

   _____

2. What is a typical workday like for you?

   _____

3. Where can I get some on-the-job experience?

   _____

4. When did you become a _____?
   (profession)

5. How much can you earn in this profession? (But remember, it's not polite to ask someone how much *he* or *she* earns.)

_____

6. Why did you choose this profession?

_____

Use a grid like the one below to keep track of the questions you ask in the boxes labeled "Q" and the answers you receive in the boxes labeled "A."

Who?	What?	Where?	When?	How?	Why?
Q	Q	Q	Q	Q	Q
A	A	A	A	A	A
Q	Q	Q	Q	Q	Q
A	A	A	A	A	A

One last suggestion: Add a professional (and very classy) touch to the interview process by following up with a thank-you note to the person who took time out of a busy schedule to talk with you.

#6 INFORMATION IS POWER

As you may have noticed, a similar pattern of information was used for each of the careers profiled in this book. Each entry included:

- ☼ a general description of the career
- ☼ Try It Out activities to give readers a chance to find out what it's really like to do each job
- ☼ a list of Web sites, library resources, and professional organizations to check for more information
- ☼ a get-acquainted interview with a professional

You may have also noticed that all the information you just gathered would fit rather nicely in a Career Ideas for Kids career profile of your own. Just fill in the blanks on the following pages to get your thoughts together (or, if this book does not belong to you, use a separate sheet of paper).

And by the way, this formula is one that you can use throughout your life to help you make fully informed career choices.

CAREER TITLE _____

WHAT IS A_____ ?

Use career encyclopedias and other resources to write a description of this career.

SKILL SET

✔ _____
✔ _____
✔ _____

_____

_____

_____

_____

 # TRY IT OUT

Write project ideas here. Ask your parents and your teacher to come up with a plan.

_____

_____

_____

_____

_____

✔ CHECK IT OUT

🖱 ON THE WEB

List Internet addresses of interesting Web sites you find.

_____

_____

_____

_____

_____

 AT THE LIBRARY

List the titles and authors of books about this career.

_____

_____

_____

_____

_____

◀ WITH THE EXPERTS

List professional organizations where you can learn more about this profession.

_____

_____

_____

_____

_____

GET ACQUAINTED

Interview a professional in the field and summarize your findings.

_____

_____

_____

_____

_____

_____

_____

WHAT'S NEXT?

Whoa, everybody! At this point, you've put in some serious miles on your career exploration journey. Before you move on, let's put things in reverse for just a sec and take another look at some of the clues you uncovered about yourself when you completed the "Discover" activities in the Get in Gear chapter on pages 7 to 26.

The following activities will help lay the clues you learned about yourself alongside the clues you learned about a favorite career idea. The comparison will help you decide if that particular career idea is a good idea for you to pursue. It doesn't matter if a certain career sounds absolutely amazing. If it doesn't honor your skills, your interests, and your values, it's not going to work for you.

The first time you looked at these activities, they were numbered one through five as "Discover" activities. This time around they are numbered in the same order but labeled "Rediscover" activities. That's not done to confuse you (sure hope it doesn't!). Instead, it's done to drive home a very important point that this is an important process you'll want to revisit time and time again as you venture throughout your career—now and later.

First, pick the one career idea that you are most interested in at this point and write its name here (or if this book doesn't belong to you, blah, blah, blah—you know the drill by now):

_____

With that idea in mind, revisit your responses to the following Get in Gear activities and complete the following:

REDISCOVER #1: WATCH FOR SIGNS ALONG THE WAY

Based on your responses to the statements on page 8, choose which of the following road signs best describes how you feel about your career idea:

- ☼ Green light—Go! Go! Go! This career idea is a perfect fit!
- ☼ Yellow light—Proceed with caution! This career idea is a good possibility, but you're not quite sure that it's the "one" just yet.
- ☼ Stop—Hit the brakes! There's no doubt about it—this career idea is definitely not for you!

REDISCOVER #2: RULES OF THE ROAD

Take another look at the work-values chart you made on page 16. Now use the same symbols to create a work-values chart for the career idea you are considering. After you have all the symbols in place, compare the two charts and answer these questions:

- ⚲ Does your career idea's **purpose** line up with yours? Would it allow you to work in the kind of **place** you most want to work in?
- ⚲ What about the **time** commitment—is it in sync with what you're hoping for?
- ⚲ Does it let you work with the **tools** and the kind of **people** you most want to work with?
- ⚲ And, last but not least, are you willing to do what it takes to **prepare** for a career like this?

PURPOSE	PLACE	TIME
TOOLS	**PEOPLE**	**PREPARATION**

REDISCOVER #3: DANGEROUS DETOURS

Go back to page 16 and double-check your list of 10 careers that you hope to avoid at any cost.

Is this career on that list? _____Yes _____ No

Should it be? _____Yes _____ No

REDISCOVER #4:
ULTIMATE CAREER DESTINATION

Pull out the ultimate career destination brochure you made (as described on page 17). Use a pencil to cross through every reference to "my ideal career" and replace it with the name of the career idea you are now considering.

Is the brochure still true? _____Yes _____ No

If not, what would you change on the brochure to make it true?

REDISCOVER #5:
GET SOME DIRECTION

Quick! Think fast! What is your personal Skill Set as discovered on page 26?

Write down your top three interest areas:

1. _____

2. _____

3. _____

What three interest areas are most closely associated with your career idea?

1. _____

2. _____

3. _____

Does this career's interest areas match any of yours?
_____Yes _____ No

Now the big question: Are you headed in the right direction?

If so, here are some suggestions to keep you moving ahead:

- ☼ Keep learning all you can about this career—read, surf the Web, talk to people, and so on. In other words, keep using some of the strategies you used in the Don't Stop Now chapter on pages 157 to 171 to do all you can to make a fully informed career decision.
- ☼ Work hard in school and get good grades. What you do now counts! Your performance, your behavior, your attitude—all conspire to either propel you forward or hold you back.
- ☼ Get involved in clubs and other after-school activities to further develop your interests and skills. Whether it's student government, 4-H, or sports, these kinds of activities give you a chance to try new things and gain confidence in your abilities.

If not, here are some suggestions to help you regroup:

- ☼ Read other books in the Career Ideas for Kids series to explore options associated with your other interest areas.
- ☼ Take a variety of classes in school and get involved in different kinds of after-school activities to get a better sense of what you like and what you do well.
- ☼ Talk to your school guidance counselor about taking a career assessment test to help fine-tune your focus.
- ☼ Most of all, remember that time is on your side. Use the next few years to discover more about yourself, explore the options, and experiment with what it will take to make you succeed. Keep at it and look forward to a fantastic future!

HOORAY! YOU DID IT!

This has been quite a trip. If someone tries to tell you that this process is easy, don't believe them. Figuring out what you want to do with the rest of your life is heavy stuff, and it should be. If you don't put some thought (and some sweat and hard work) into the process, you'll get stuck with whatever comes your way.

You may not have things planned to a T. Actually, it's probably better if you don't. You'll change some of your ideas as you grow and experience new things. And, you may find an interesting detour or two along the way. That's okay.

The most important thing about beginning this process now is that you've started to dream. You've discovered that you have some unique talents and abilities to share. You've become aware of some of the ways you can use them to make a living—and perhaps make a difference in the world.

Whatever you do, don't lose sight of the hopes and dreams you've discovered. You've got your entire future ahead of you. Use it wisely.

PASSPORT TO YOUR FUTURE

Getting where you want to go requires patience, focus, and lots of hard work. It also hinges on making good choices. Following is a list of some surefire ways to give yourself the best shot at a bright future. Are you up to the challenge? Can you do it? Do you dare?

Put your initials next to each item that you absolutely promise to do.

____ ☼ Do my best in every class at school
____ ☼ Take advantage of every opportunity to get a wide variety of experiences through participation in sports, after-school activities, at my favorite place of worship, and in my community
____ ☼ Ask my parents, teachers, or other trusted adults for help when I need it
____ ☼ Stay away from drugs, alcohol, and other bad scenes that can rob me of a future before I even get there
____ ☼ Graduate from high school

SOME FUTURE DESTINATIONS

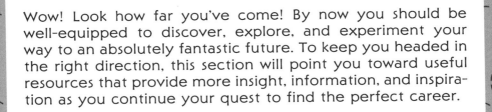

Wow! Look how far you've come! By now you should be well-equipped to discover, explore, and experiment your way to an absolutely fantastic future. To keep you headed in the right direction, this section will point you toward useful resources that provide more insight, information, and inspiration as you continue your quest to find the perfect career.

IT'S NOT JUST FOR NERDS

The school counselor's office is not just a place where teachers send troublemakers. One of its main purposes is to help students like you make the most of your educational opportunities. Most schools will have a number of useful resources, including career assessment tools (ask about the Self-Directed Search Career Explorer or the COPS Interest

Inventory—these are especially useful assessments for people your age). They may also have a stash of books, videos, and other helpful materials.

Make sure no one's looking and sneak into your school counseling office to get some expert advice!

AWESOME INTERNET CAREER RESOURCES

Your parents will be green with envy when they see all the career planning resources you have at your fingertips. Get ready to hear them whine, "But they didn't have all this stuff when I was a kid." Make the most of these cyberspace opportunities.

☼ **Adventures in Education**
http://adventuresineducation.org/middleschool
Here you'll find some useful tools to make the most of your education—starting now. Make sure to watch "The Great College Mystery," an online animation featuring Dr. Ed.

☼ **America's Career InfoNet**
http://www.acinet.org
Career sites don't get any bigger than this one! Compliments of the U.S. Department of Labor, and a chunk of your parent's tax dollars, you'll find all kinds of information about what people do, how much money they make, and where they work. Although it's mostly geared toward adults, you may want to take a look at some of the videos (the site has links to more than 450!) that show people at work.

☼ **ASVAB Career Exploration Program**
http://www.asvabprogram.com
This site may prove especially useful as you continue to think through various options. It includes sections

for students to learn about themselves, to explore careers, and to plan for their futures.

☼ Career Voyages
http://www.careervoyages.gov
This site will be especially helpful to you as you get a little older. It offers four paths to get you started: "Where do I start?" "Which industries are growing?" "How do I qualify and get a job?" and "Does education pay? How do I pay?" However, it also includes a special section especially for elementary school students. Just click the button that says "Still in elementary school?" or go to http://www.careervoyages .gov/students-elementary.cfm.

☼ Job Profiles
http://jobprofiles.org
This site presents the personal side of work with profiles of people working in jobs associated with agriculture and nature, arts and sports, business and communications, construction and manufacturing, education and science, government, health and social services, retail and wholesale, and other industries.

☼ Major and Careers Central
http://www.collegeboard.com/csearch/majors_careers
This site is hosted by the College Board (the organization responsible for a very important test called the SAT, which you're likely to encounter if you plan to go to college). It includes helpful information about how different kinds of subjects you can study in college can prepare you for specific types of jobs.

☼ Mapping Your Future
http://mapping-your-future.org/MHSS

This site provides strategies and resources for students as they progress through middle school and high school.

☼ My Cool Career
http://www.mycoolcareer.com
This site is where you can take free online self-assessment quizzes, explore your dreams, and listen to people with interesting jobs talk about their work.

☼ O*NET Online
http://online.onetcenter.org
This U.S. Department of Labor site provides comprehensive information about hundreds of important occupations. Although you may need to ask a parent or teacher to help you figure out how to use the system, it can be a good source of digging for nitty-gritty details about a specific type of job. For instance, each profile includes a description of the skills, abilities, and special knowledge needed to perform each job.

☼ Think College Early
http://www.ed.gov/students/prep/college
thinkcollege/early/edlite-tcehome.html
Even though you almost need a college degree just to type the Web address for this U.S. Department of Education site, it contains some really cool career information and helps you think about how college might fit into your future plans.

☼ What Interests You?
http://www.bls.gov/k12
This Bureau of Labor Statistics site is geared toward students. It lets you explore careers by interests such as reading, building and fixing things, managing money, helping people, and more.

JOIN THE CLUB

Once you've completed eighth grade, you are eligible to check out local opportunities to participate in Learning for Life's career education programs. Some communities offer Explorer posts that sponsor activities with students interested in industries that include the arts and humanities, aviation, business, communications, engineering, fire service, health, law enforcement, law and government, science, skilled trades, or social services. To find a local office, go to http://www.learning-for-life.org/exploring/main.html and type your zip code.

Until then, you can go online and play *Life Choices*, a really fun and challenging game where you get one of five virtual jobs at http://www.learning-for-life.org/games/LCSH/index.html.

MORE CAREER BOOKS ESPECIALLY FOR KIDS

It's especially important that people your age find out all they can about as many different careers as they can. Books like the ones listed below can introduce all kinds of interesting ideas that you might not encounter in your everyday life.

Greenfeld, Barbara C., and Robert A. Weinstein. *The Kids' College Almanac: A First Look at College*. 3d ed. Indianapolis, Ind.: JIST Works, 2005.
Young Person's Occupational Outlook Handbook. Indianapolis, Ind.: JIST Works, 2005.

Following are brief descriptions of several series of books geared especially toward kids like you. To find copies of these books, ask your school or public librarian to help you search the library computer system using the name of the series.

Career Connections (published by UXL)
This extensive series features information and illustrations
   about jobs of interest to people interested in art and design,
   entrepreneurship, food, government and law, history, math
   and computers, and the performing arts as well as those who
   want to work with their hands or with living things.

Career Ideas for Kids (written by Diane Lindsey Reeves, published by Ferguson)
This series of interactive career exploration books features 10
   different titles for kids who like adventure and travel, animals
   and nature, art, computers, math and money, music and
   dance, science, sports, talking, and writing.

Careers Without College (published by Peterson's)
These books offer a look at options available to those who
   prefer to find jobs that do not require a college degree and
   include titles focusing on cars, computers, fashion, fitness,
   health care, and music.

Cool Careers (published by Rosen Publishing)
Each title in this series focuses on a cutting-edge occupation
   such as computer animator, hardware engineer, multimedia
   and new media developer, video game designer, Web entrepreneur, and webmaster.

Discovering Careers for Your Future (published by Ferguson)
This series includes a wide range of titles that include those
   that focus on adventure, art, construction, fashion, film, history, nature, publishing, and radio and television.

Risky Business (written by Keith Elliot Greenberg, published by
   Blackbirch Press)
These books feature stories about people with adventurous
   types of jobs and include titles about a bomb squad officer,
   disease detective, marine biologist, photojournalist, rodeo
   clown, smoke jumper, storm chaser, stunt woman, test pilot,
   and wildlife special agent.

HEAVY-DUTY RESOURCES

Career encyclopedias provide general information about a lot of professions and can be a great place to start a career search. Those listed here are easy to use and provide useful information about nearly a zillion different jobs. Look for them in the reference section of your local library.

Career Discovery Encyclopedia, 6th ed. New York: Ferguson, 2006.

Careers for the 21st Century. Farmington Hills, Mich.: Lucent Books, 2002.

Children's Dictionary of Occupations. Princeton, N.J.: Cambridge Educational, 2004.

Encyclopedia of Career and Vocational Guidance. New York: Ferguson, 2005.

Farr, Michael, and Laurence Shatkin. *Enhanced Occupational Outlook Handbook.* 6th ed. Indianapolis, Ind.: JIST Works, 2006.

Occupational Outlook Handbook. Washington, D.C.: U.S. Government Printing Office, 2006.

FINDING PLACES TO WORK

Even though you probably aren't quite yet in the market for a real job, you can learn a lot about the kinds of jobs you might find if you were looking by visiting some of the most popular job-hunting sites on the Internet. Two particularly good ones to investigate are America's Job Bank (http://www.ajb.org) and Monster (http://www.monster.com).

INDEX

Page numbers in **boldface** indicate main articles. Page numbers in *italics* indicate photographs.